BARRON'S BOOK NOTES

GEOFFREY CHAUCER'S

Canterbury Tales

BY

Cynthia C. Werthamer
Instructor
Bloomfield College
Bloomfield, New Jersey

SERIES EDITOR

Michael Spring
Editor, *Literary Cavalcade*
Scholastic Inc.

BARRON'S EDUCATIONAL SERIES, INC.

*Thanks to Holly Hughes,
Meredith Gang, and
Michael Bergmann; and
especially to Felice Nudelman.*

ACKNOWLEDGMENTS

We would like to acknowledge the many painstaking hours of work
Holly Hughes and Thomas F. Hirsch have devoted to making the
Book Notes series a success.

All inquiries should be addressed to:
Barron's Educational Series, Inc.
250 Wireless Boulevard
Hauppauge, New York 11788

Library of Congress Catalog Card No. 84-18489

International Standard Book No. 0-8120-3406-6

Library of Congress Cataloging in Publication Data
Werthamer, Cynthia C.
  Geoffrey Chaucer's Canterbury Tales.

  (Barron's book notes)
  Bibliography: p. 118
  Summary: A guide to reading "Canterbury Tales" with
a critical and appreciative mind. Includes background
on the author's life and times, sample tests, term paper
suggestions, and a reading list.
  1. Chaucer, Geoffrey, d. 1400. Canterbury tales.
[1. Chaucer, Geoffrey, c. 1400. Canterbury tales.
2. English literature—History and criticism] I. Title.
PR1874.W4   1984   821'.1   84-18489
ISBN 0-8120-3406-6 (pbk.)

CONTENTS

THE AUTHOR AND HIS TIMES

Most people in the English society of Chaucer's time, about 600 years ago, viewed the world in a similar way and accepted the same beliefs. People then believed that behind the chaos and frustration of the day-to-day world there was a divine providence that gave a reason to everything, even though that reason wasn't always obvious. When you've got faith in an overall system like that, it's easier to accept and understand the world around you. People in Chaucer's society could feel, at least much of the time, a sense of security about the world, knowing that it was following a divine plan. They trusted the system they believed in; it was true, and they felt no need to question it.

So behind all of Chaucer's satire and social put-downs in the *Canterbury Tales* is an unshaken belief in a divine order. It's easier to make fun of something when, underneath, you know you take it seriously. Also, as Chaucer knew, it's easier to write for a group of people who at least roughly share the same set of values, whether they be a cook, a parson, or an upper-class prioress.

Those values were represented in the medieval world by two structures: the class system and the church. People believed both setups were established by God, and each went unchallenged. A peasant, like Chaucer's Plowman, wasn't "upwardly mobile" as in our society, and didn't aspire to become a knight. He may want to buy more horses or farm more land, but he wouldn't change his basic lifestyle or his station in life.

In the Middle Ages, each person was classified according to his or her "estate" or place on the social scale depending on birth, profession, and other factors (such as whether a woman was married—an important discussion of which is in the Wife of Bath's Tale as well as others). Each social grouping was like a symbol of the divine order, as immune to change as the hierarchy of angels. That's why a move from the peasant to the middle class, for example, was almost unheard of.

The middle class was in its infancy then. Chaucer himself was a member of what we'd call the upper middle class; he got jobs at court without actually being royalty. He started out as a page, serving meals and learning the ropes of becoming a courtly gentleman. He also quickly found out about the conflicting whims of human nature and the importance of the right appearances, both lessons he draws on in the *Canterbury Tales.* He evidently learned them well in real life, too, because he became a diplomat and traveled for the king to France and Italy, where he picked up plenty of literary influences that show up in the *Canterbury Tales* and other works.

Chaucer uses class structure very clearly in the *Tales*, presenting the Knight first and having him tell the first tale because he's the highest-ranking pilgrim present. The nobility, being at the top of the social scale, was responsible for cultivating virtue, keeping the peace by maintaining social order, and setting a moral example for the other classes to follow.

Apart from the worldly order but just as important was the church hierarchy. It, too, was a structure ordained by God (especially since everyone in the church was Roman Catholic in the hundreds of years before Martin Luther and the Reformation). Yet within the church ranks there was incredible in-fighting between the "regular" clergy (those in convents and monasteries, like the Monk, Prioress, and Friar in the *Tales*) and the "secular" clergy (parish priests like the Parson and eventually perhaps the Clerk). Each section was, in a sense, feuding with the other for "turf." Chaucer exemplifies this by showing an argument between the Pardoner (a church official of the secular variety) and the Friar, who is in direct competition with the Pardoner for money and religious influence over the parish villages they both travel through.

The regular clergy, in particular, had a reputation for corruption at that time. Monasteries, which were supposed to be apart from the world and whose inhabitants were to avoid worldly goods, were almost as lavish as castles by the 14th century, and most people assumed that friars (like Chaucer's picture of one) kept much of the money they were supposed to give to the poor. At one point in his life Chaucer lived in a part of London that was very near several large monastic orders, and he probably got to see a good deal of their life and work. He also, as we can see from his history, had little sympathy for cheating clerics. In fact, he was once fined for beating up a friar outside a courthouse!

Yet people still gave money to friars and pardoners because you could never be too sure. Even if the friar or pardoner were corrupt, giving to charity or buying a papal pardon could still help get you into heaven or at least knock a few thousand years off your stay in purgatory. Also, just because a friar or monk was a less-than-sterling example of his station, the social position itself still commanded respect.

What about the importance of pilgrimages, which certainly are important in Chaucer's *Tales*? You must realize, first of all, that pilgrims were ordinary people, not even necessarily very religious (as you can see from the Prologue), who visited religious shrines as much for a holiday as for the heavenly benefits. Such trips even took on the qualities of holidays at the shrines, with people like Chaucer's Pardoner selling holy "relics", and souvenir stands set up along the route. For some people, like the Wife of Bath, it was the only way to escape the pressures of home, especially for a woman. (We suspect that the Wife may be along for other reasons as well.) Spring was a particularly popular pilgrimage time in England, and Chaucer duly begins this report of a pilgrimage with a description of the spring.

It's also not unusual to have a large, oddly assorted mixture of people heading out on a pilgrimage together, sort of a medieval tour bus. Travel was slow, roads were rutted, and there were highway robbers, accidents, and illness. Then, as now, there's company and comfort in numbers, so why travel alone when you could travel with others, especially if they told such entertaining stories? Because of the festive atmosphere of many pilgrimages, some clerics frowned on them, but neither Chaucer nor his pilgrims cares about such matters.

By using the format of a pilgrimage, however, Chaucer reminds us that behind all the jokes are the serious truths that he and his pilgrims believed in. Amid the clamor of different characters and different points of view, he's reminding us that earthly truth has as many aspects as there are pilgrims, and that the pilgrims are trying to find a single truth that is impossible for mortals to find. It doesn't matter that the tales are chaotic and unfinished; what matters is that God's truth existed for Chaucer beyond the chaos of every-day lives and explanations.

A Note on This Guide

Although Chaucer did not complete the *Canterbury Tales*, he managed to write 24 of them, plus the General Prologue and a Retraction. Not every character mentioned in the Prologue has a tale, and no character gets to tell the two tales that Chaucer intended each to deliver. Even so, most editions of the *Canterbury Tales* that you'll come across include a limited number of the 24 tales.

This guide presents and analyzes in depth the five tales most often read, plus the General Prologue. These are the five you are most likely to be reading and studying. They are representative of Chaucer's varied styles. The Knight's Tale is often considered to be Chaucer's best romance; the Miller's Tale, his funniest; the Wife of Bath's Prologue and Tale, his best-drawn characterization; the Pardoner's Tale, an excellent allegory and study in contrast between pilgrim and tale; and the Nun's Priest's Tale, a clear philosophical statement and a wonderfully charming mock-heroic fable. As for the General Prologue, most students know that it's essential reading as an introduction to the *Canterbury Tales*.

The other tales—though not treated here in depth, and not read as often in the classroom—certainly have their merits.

These other tales are presented in summary, following the in-depth presentations, and for each, special elements are highlighted that deserve consideration when you read the stories.

THE POEM

The old saying goes, "In spring a young man's fancy turns to thoughts of love." For Chaucer, who opens the General Prologue to the *Canterbury Tales* with a wonderful description of spring, this was the time when people longed "to go on pilgrimages."

On that sunny April day, "Chaucer" (coincidentally the name Chaucer chose for his narrator) happens to be at the Tabard Inn in Southwark, just south of London. He's going on his own pilgrimage to the cathedral at Canterbury where St. Thomas à Becket preached and was murdered. By chance, 29 other pilgrims come trooping into the tavern, also headed for Canterbury. Chaucer chats with all of them, becomes part of their group, and decides to leave with them early the next morning. Chaucer then tells us all about the group he's joined: who they are, what their station in life is, even what they're wearing. He proceeds to give us detailed descriptions of almost all of them, starting with the Knight, the highest-ranking member of the group.

The Host then feeds the pilgrims plenty of food and wine, and takes the floor. He knows that the holiday mood of a pilgrimage means people will laugh and joke along the way. He has a plan; how many people will agree to it? They cheerfully agree, and the Host proposes that each pilgrim should tell two tales on the way to Canterbury and two more on the way back. Whoever tells the best tale—the most morally instructive as well as the most amusing (see Note)—gets treated to dinner by the rest of the gang on the return trip (at the Host's inn, of course).

Early next morning, the group heads out and the Host has everyone draw straws to see who will tell the first tale. The Knight picks the shortest straw, and the Prologue ends as the Knight prepares to speak.

NOTE: The scheme of two stories out, two back was never completed by Chaucer. Instruction plus amusement were the criteria by which good stories were judged in Chaucer's day. Originality was not important, but embellishment, and how well a story was adapted, were highly valued.

It is fitting that the Knight, "by cas" (by chance) picks to go first, as he is the highest in the social hierarchy on the trip. Chaucer is saying the choice seems random, but is not. This idea resurfaces throughout the *Tales*.

The Pilgrims

The major characters in the General Prologue are the very people who soon will be telling *their* stories with *other* characters in them. So keep in mind that Chaucer's description of each character tells us something about the character's personality, but that we'll also learn something more about the character based on the story he or she tells. (After our picture of the Miller, for example, we're not surprised that he tells a dirty story.) We get further hints from the prologues to each person's story.

Chaucer tells us much about each pilgrim, not only by telling us what they do for a living, but also through description of their clothes, attitudes, even their bodies. His medieval audience would compare Chaucer's descriptions against the social stereotypes they knew already about each person's profession or "station." Chaucer's list of attributes often parodies the standards set for a given rank, turning some descriptions into great comedy.

The Knight

The Knight is everything an archetypal medieval knight should be: "worthy" (distinguished), and loving chivalry, truth, honor, "freedom" (selflessness), and courtesy. There's no irony here. He is "ever honored" for his bravery. He's quite literally been through the wars; his tunic is still stained by his chain-mail armor because he's heading on his pilgrimage straight from his latest Crusade. He's "gentil" (well bred), "verray" (true), in short, "parfit" (perfect). Chaucer uses all the conventional descriptions because the Knight is what every knight should be, but usually isn't.

We hear more about the Knight's 15 "mortal battles" than about his appearance, since his actions are more important than his looks. (All we know besides his tunic is that he is not gaudily dressed and has "good" horses.) His actions are more important to his audience (who, like us, are excited by news of foreign wars and travel) and also to his own code of knightly behavior. Keep this in mind during his Tale, which deals with two other worthy knights whose behavior dictates who will win or lose the lady they both love.

The Squire

The Squire is a young man of about 20, not yet as mature as his father. He is a "lover" and "lusty bachelor," which meant a young man aspiring to knighthood. His hair is curled as though it had been set—telling us he is more concerned than his father about appearances—and he places importance on fighting for his lady's honor, not, like his father, for abstract ideals or God. Squires were apprenticed to knights before they could become knights (even King Arthur was one), which is why this Squire is "courteous, humble," and carves meat at his father's table. He can sing and dance, joust, and write songs and poems— all important social accomplishments for a young man of his rank. He wears stylish but daring clothing—a short gown (equivalent in shock value to a miniskirt)—which would not be viewed kindly by priests warning against stylish clothing.

It's been said that Chaucer didn't like the Squire. because of the young man's emphasis on vanity and pretty things, but the description, even the curls, is the standard romance convention for young heroes. (Don't forget, the Squire also is very agile and "of great strength.") And the last couplet tells that he's courteous and well bred. True to his nature, his tale tells of Gawain, a knight of King Arthur's court, and the magical gifts he bestows in a foreign land. The tale may have gone on to speak of the Squire's other main interest, love, but we'll never know because Chaucer left it unfinished. (He does mention the love of a falcon for her lost mate, though.) We get another view of the Squire's good breeding in a compliment from the Franklin, who wishes his own son were more Squire-like.

NOTE: The Squire is intentionally compared to the description of spring at the beginning of the Prologue. His clothes are embroidered like a meadow, "al ful of fresshe floures, whyte and rede," and he is "fresh as is the month of May." Like the birds sleeping with open eyes, he sleeps "namore than dooth a nightingale" because of his high spirits and energy. He is of nature, rather than of the "higher" orders of reason and thought like the Knight, but there's hope. After all, he's still young.

The Yeoman

The Knight's servant (or assistant) is dressed in green, has bright peacock-feather arrows in his belt, and a "mighty bow" in his hand, so Chaucer guesses he's a forester and hunter when not attending the Knight. He also wears a medal of St. Christopher, patron saint of foresters, around his neck. He's obviously proud of his abilities since he takes care not to let his arrow feathers droop.

The Prioress

Some believe the Prioress is a woman on whom Chaucer (or at least the narrator) had a crush. It certainly seems so from the description of her, which is more fitting to a beloved lady in a romance than to a nun. The description makes it seem that she's a gentlewoman, who possibly entered a convent because she had no marriage dowry. Her smile is "simple and coy" (modest and sweet), words that come straight out of a romance, as Chaucer's audience would instantly recognize. She doesn't curse (or at least, only slightly, by "St. Loy," who happens to have been a handsome courtier before he turned to religion). Even her name, "Madame Eglentyne," meaning "sweet briar," is a demure one that appears in several popular romances. Again, Chaucer refers to a beautiful worldly heroine, implying behavior that is far from nunlike. But is she evil, just because she speaks French very well, has perfect table manners, and likes being proper? She is "so charitable" that she would weep "if she saw a mouse caught in a trap." Some think this implies that she cares more about animals' suffering than people, especially in the light of the tale she calmly tells about the way the Jews are punished for supposedly killing a Christian child. She also keeps small dogs as pets (strictly forbidden in a convent) and feeds them the finest meat, milk, and bread.

NOTE: Notice how here and elsewhere Chaucer shifts from describing the person to being inside his or her head. He hasn't seen Madame Eglentyne cry over a mouse, or feed her dogs, yet he describes exactly how she does it.

The description of her table manners comes straight from the French *Romance of the Rose*, which Chaucer translated and which his audience would have known. The joke here is that in the romance this description is from a scene on how women attract and keep lovers! In fact, it is ironic that the Prioress is along on a pilgrimage, since she should have remained inside the cloister walls.

Her physical description, too, comes straight from French romances. Chaucer uses every cliché in the book: her nose is "tretys" (shapely), her eyes "grey as glass," her mouth "small, soft and red." Her forehead, which technically shouldn't even be visible in a nun's habit, is fair and broad, a style so fashionable that women in Chaucer's day used to pluck their hairlines to make their foreheads larger. Perhaps most intriguing of all, she wears a large gold brooch (jewelry is forbidden in convents) that reads, *Amor vincit omnia* ("love conquers all"). It's not clear how Chaucer means us to interpret the phrase. The original motto (from Virgil) referred to earthly love, but it was used by the medieval church to mean God's love. How does the Prioress interpret it? It's possible that she would think only of the godly connotations, but some readers believe the double meaning is no accident. The Prioress retains some vanities of her preconvent days, but does Chaucer intend to show her as a hypocrite? Or, because of her lack of charity, as intentionally cruel? Certainly she is not everything a nun should be—compare her in idealism to the Knight—but you can also find a great deal of affection in Chaucer's picture of her. Isn't it understandable that a well-bred young woman should want to keep some of the innocent pleasures of worldly life in a convent? Reforming bishops often warned even heads of convents against keeping pets and wearing jewelry, but the frequency of the warnings indicates they were pretty much ignored.

The Monk

The Monk's description is the first that is really noticeably sarcastic. Monks are supposed to stay apart from the world, not go out for "venery" (hunting)—a word that, along with Venus, carries sexual connotations, since it also means "hunting" women. All the comparisons are ironic: his bridle bells are as clear as the chapel bell he's supposed to be in charge of; his face seems "anointed" like one of the blessed, which he's clearly not; he's not "pale as a ghost" or spirit, which a monk should be. There's a "love knot" under his chin, which Chaucer, ever polite, merely calls "curious" (downright suspicious might be more like it).

The narrator naïvely agrees with the monk, or pretends to, that there's no earthly reason to sweat over books or manual labor as decreed by St. Augustine, founder of the Monk's order. The Monk, in saying this, knows (more than the Prioress does) he's going against his calling. Others know it, too, for the Host, in the Monk's Prologue, teases the Monk that he doesn't look like one, but more like someone in charge of the food and drink, or like a rooster with plenty of hens. This reinforces the piggish, selfish picture we have of him. The Monk takes it in stride and tells a tale, actually several, describing the ups and downs of fortune's wheel in the lives of Satan, Adam, Hercules, and others—so boringly that the Knight begs him to stop and the Host asks him to discuss hunting instead. Does the company and Chaucer see more about the Monk than he sees of himself? There is evidence in the way he talks, in the way he seems to believe it's pointless to follow his monastic duties. But you could also find ways of showing that while the Monk is stupid about his priorities, he is not truly evil, just misguided.

The Friar

The Friar is "wanton and merry," but this pleasant-sounding description is dripping with sarcasm. By the 14th century, friars, who were supposed to give up all worldly things and live only by begging for food and alms, were almost totally corrupt. They were known for flattering the rich and deceiving the poor, and especially for seducing women in outright disregard for their vow of celibacy.

Chaucer's Friar, Hubert, is a "limitour," one who is licensed to beg in a certain area. If the Monk's portrait contains veiled sexual innuendoes, Hubert's are blatant. He is "ful solempne" (very impressive) because he knows so much about "daliaunce" (small talk or flirtation). He's married off women "at his owene cost"—implying that he seduced them first. He's "well beloved and familiar" with "worthy women" of his area. We can imagine what that means. He's allowed to hear confessions and gives easy penances if he knows he'll get well paid. Chaucer comments here on the hypocrisy of society, too, in saying sarcastically that people can give money to "poor friars" to atone for their sins instead of "weeping and praying."

It gets worse. Hubert keeps trinkets to give pretty wives (like the present-day picture of a traveling salesman). He knows all the bars and is more familiar with barmaids and innkeepers than the lepers or beggars he's supposed to be soliciting for. (Ideally, after buying necessities, friars were supposed to donate to the poor and sick any leftover money from begging.) Sharpening the irony, Chaucer says it's not right for someone of Hubert's profession ("facultee") to be acquainted with lepers, since after all there's no money there. But when it comes to the rich and the food sellers, suddenly he's "curteis" and humble. So much for Christian charity. His "In principio" (Bible recitation) is so pleasant that he can always get a farthing (or "fair thing," another sexual reference); he gets more money from his illegal takings ("purchas") than his legal "rente." He wears clothes better suited to a pope than to the "poor scholar" he's supposed to be, and he meddles in "love-days," which were assigned for settling civil disputes out of court. Friars were allowed to represent the poor, otherwise they were under strict orders not to interfere. Hubert even lisps to make his English sound more appealing, presumably to women. Is he "worthy"—as Chaucer calls him (*line 270*)—in the same way the Knight is worthy, or is Chaucer's last line of description the final underlining irony? Obviously, Hubert is everything that a friar shouldn't be—corrupt, rich, greedy, and lecherous— and the tale he later tells reinforces this. He tells of a corrupt summoner (an officer who orders people to appear in court) whose behavior involves trickery, lies, and violence—strikingly similar to the Friar's own nature. The summoner gets dragged off by the Devil. Are we to believe that the Friar is headed the same way?

The Merchant

The Merchant's description is short but telling. You might recognize him: the wealthy businessman who puts up an impressive, expensive front but who is hiding the fact that he is in debt. With the Merchant, Chaucer begins reports of three men who live by "reson," even though the Merchant and Sergeant of Law's "resons" deal more with money than truth, as the Clerk does.

The Merchant wears a Flemish hat, a "motley" (variously colored) coat, and well-fastened boots. That he's an individual is clear even from so few lines: his hat is distinctive for his time and class, his remarks are solemn, and his "governaunce" (manner) dignified. But he is typical in scathing ways. He always talks about increasing his profits, a sin not only of greed but of pride, and worse, he deals in "chevyssaunce," moneylending for interest, which was illegal. He's concerned with protecting the ocean trade routes between Holland and England. You would be, too, if you staked your fortune as he does on the English wool you exported to the Continent. He also ignores the law against "eschaunge" (exchange). It was illegal for private citizens to buy and sell foreign currency (in this case, French gold coins)—out of fear of inflation, much like now—but unscrupulous merchants did it anyway. No wonder Chaucer said he didn't know the Merchant's name! If he based him on a real person, it probably wouldn't be a smart idea to poke public fun at a powerful man to whom many people owe money. We learn more about the Merchant in the Prologue to his tale. He's been married only two months; his tale therefore deals with the idea of a well-balanced marriage.

The Clerk

But if the Merchant's picture is somewhat tainted, we get a sense of great affection for the Clerk, a man after Chaucer's own heart who spends his money on books. He looks thin and studious, the way the Monk and Friar ought to look but don't. Even his horse is lean "as a rake." He is studying for the priesthood, but doesn't yet have a living (benefice) from it, and is too pious to take secular "office." He's a philosopher who borrows money for books.

NOTE: "*Philosopher*" also meant "alchemist," one who tries to make gold from lead. Some readers see parallels between this Clerk and the lecherous clerk

Nicholas in the Miller's Tale, who also keeps books by his bed, whose interests are alchemy and lust. Decide for yourself whether the analogy is fair.

Some see a greediness in the Clerk's book buying because they are fine volumes with "blak and rede" bindings. (At least he remembers to pray for those he borrows from!) Unlike some of the other pilgrims, he never speaks "more than was nede," but when he does he speaks well, with "moral virtu." Before he tells his tale later, in fact, the Host teases him for being so quiet. His tale about the worthy Griselde, deals with the virtues of patience and "a stiff upper lip" in the face of disappointment.

The Sergeant of the Law

A barrister of high standing appointed by the king, he somehow gets demoted to merely a *Man of Law* (plain lawyer) in the actual tale-telling. But in the Prologue he is "ful riche of excellence," discreet, and wise, or at least he seems to be because of his impressive style. Might this imply that like the Merchant he is less than he appears? There is evidence for this, since

> Nowher so bisy a man as he ther nas,
> And yet he semed bisier than he was.
>
> *(lines 323–324)*

He is able to purchase land "fee simple"—flat out—because of his insider's knowledge, and can find and close any loophole. He spends time at the "parvys," the portal of St. Paul's Cathedral in London where lawyers often met to discuss cases. His list of accomplishments reads like a résumé, and he knows every case since William the Conqueror.

In making his material success so obvious and detailed, Chaucer implies that the man has little to show as a human being. But lawyers in the Middle Ages generally had reputations as poor as they do now, and preachers had a field day chewing out lawyers almost as much as friars for their price-gouging and attempts to increase their gains. Ironically, in introducing his tale, the Man of Law protests he will tell a story in prose because he's a plain-speaking man. (And after all that, it's not in prose!) He tells a tale of a Sultan's conversion to Christianity in order to marry, and the sufferings he and his wife undergo before they are reunited—a completed contract, as it were.

The Franklin

The wealthy landowner, the Franklin is one of Chaucer's most colorful characters, literally. His beard is white as a daisy, a symbol of earthly or heavenly love. Here, it's earthly all right. Earthy, too, as the Franklin delights in food and pleasure as "felicitee parfyt" (perfect happiness). But this portrait isn't sarcastic, as are the Monk's and Friar's, since the Franklin's station in life is to be a generous good neighbor. Elected a knight of the shire many times (Chaucer was one himself), the Franklin is "Seint Julien," patron saint of hospitality, in his neck of the woods. He's held other public offices as well, and he is almost the social equal of the Sergeant of the Law. A "sangwen" complexion (sanguine disposition) was one of the four "humors" believed to govern the body, in this case, outgoing and hearty. He carries out his part in life, "Epicurus [who personified pleasure] owene son." Even as he introduces his tale about "trouthe" in marriage, he notes that the only "colors" he knows are not

descriptive, just the ones he sees in the meadow—
such as daisies!

The Five Tradesmen

The Haberdasher, Carpenter, Weaver, Dyer, and
Tapestry Maker are doing well. Their wives wish they
were aldermen; they would love to be called "madame" and be honored by entering the church first.
This is a vivid picture of rather petty men, although
the guilds to which they belonged were important
union-type groups that supported restoration work
on churches and other significant social functions.
Guilds had enough political power so that their members could easily have had enough land to be elected
aldermen.

The Cook

The Cook is an excellent chef, but less excellent a
human being. He "knowe a draughte of Londoun
ale" perhaps too well, and the real giveaway is the
"mormal" (open sore) on his shin, which is unappe-
tizing and might be syphilitic. His evident bad habits
are reinforced by the tale he tells, unfinished, about
an unsavory young cook who corrupts others with his
bad habits.

The Shipman

The Shipman knows his seafaring business and
tides and routes, inside and out. Chaucer admires his
skills because England's strength as a medieval super-
power depended on its navy. But "of nice conscience
took he no keep," and he's not above watering down
the wine he brings from Bordeaux for men like the
Merchant and the Tradesmen. He's not averse to killing either, sending his prisoners "hoom to every
lond" by water, i.e., overboard. His tale is of a monk

who is as much of a pirate as he is himself, abusing the hospitality of a kindly merchant.

The Doctor of Physik

He is a "verray, parfit" practitioner of his art, but is he "true and perfect" in the same way that the Knight is? Certainly he is very learned, familiar with all the ancient and modern physicians (including some who, according to his time and place, he shouldn't have even heard of!). He knows astrology, which was considered a respectable science in Chaucer's day, although some conservatives were against it as anti-Christian. He knows every patient's humor" and can help align the patient with favorable astrological signs.

NOTE: The four humors—"hot" (choleric), "cold" (melancholy), "moiste" (sanguine, like the Franklin), and watery (phlegmatic)—were believed to rule the body, and an excess of one created illness.

The Doctor by medieval standards is no quack, but he is suspicious. He has arrangements with "apothecaries" (druggists) who help him make a profit. Some doctors and pharmacists, then as now, were accused of overcharging patients on prescriptions and then splitting the difference. The Doctor also knows "but litel on the Bible," a sure sign that his knowledge, even though it encompasses the stars, is restricted to the lower "physical" things in life, since it doesn't contain God.

Finally, Chaucer says sweetly, he's saved all the money he's made from the plagues that were common in the Middle Ages, "For gold in phisyk is a cordial [medicine]. Therefor he lovede gold in special" (*lines 41-446*). Is this the only reason he loves gold, because it's a good medicine? Look at the way he's dressed, in taffeta and "sendal" (silk); that should give you a clue. His tale, which he tells us deals with the price of sin, is of an unjust judge who lies to get the woman he wants. The woman, Virginia, is so honorable, however, that she dies rather than submit to him. In keeping with the Doctor's profession, he gives a long hymn to nature for forming that perfect machine, the body.

The Wife of Bath

She is one of Chaucer's most lively inventions. She thinks very highly of herself and her skill as a weaver (better even than the renowned Belgians). She lets us know she's entitled to make the first offering at church services, an honor carrying great social prestige. (But watch out if you cut in front of her, then she won't give a penny.) She shows off her Sunday clothes with evident pride, including "ten pounds" of "coverchiefs," finely textured veils arranged over her head. Her clothing tells us she is no shy, retiring wallflower.

But we're more interested in her famous love life than in her fashions. She's had five husbands—later, in her Prologue to the tale she tells, she gives the histories of all five—not to mention "other company in youth." (But, says Chaucer, we don't have to mention that. Is he perhaps embarrassed?) She's an old hand at pilgrimages, and, it's implied, the loose morals that sometimes go along; she knows, probably in both senses, "muche of wandring by the weye." She's gaptoothed, a medieval sign that some believe had to do with sexual accomplishment, or with a bold, faithless nature, or with traveling. The Wife of Bath, we find out, has plenty of all three.

Her tale deals not surprisingly with the upper hand a woman must maintain in marriage. She is "somdel [somewhat] deaf," but that doesn't stop her from amorous adventures; she also later gives more detail about her "other company" that Chaucer passes lightly over by saying,

> Of remedies of love she knew per chaunce,
> For she koude [knew] of that art the olde
> daunce.

> *(lines 475–476)*

The "remedies of love" implies she knows of Ovid's ancient work of the same name, which deals with all the rules of the love game. The idea of knowing the rules of the game, especially of a sexual nature, shows up often in reference to the Wife.

Is she meant to be purely ironic? It wouldn't be strange to Chaucer's audience to hear of five husbands, since no woman, especially one with property and one as willing as the Wife, would stay a widow for long. She uses all her "reson" for defending the delights of the lower regions of the body. But can you find anything in her portrait that cuts, for example, like the knife Chaucer uses against the Doctor? The Wife is teased, but is she judged? More than any other character, Chaucer lets her speak for herself.

The Parson

The poor Parson, like the Knight, is the ideal of what someone of his class ought to be. He is "lerned," "in adversitee ful [very] pacient," and is a "noble ensaumple" (example) to his parishioners. Given what we've already seen of learned men and their abuses, it's unusual that this one should possess such virtue—he is even "loath" to collect his "tithes" (income tax on which he lives). He practices what he preaches, knowing that he must set the example for the common people, "For if a preest be foul, on whom we truste, No wonder is a lewed [ignorant] man to ruste" *(lines 503–504)* like "iren." He doesn't, like some priests, run to London and rent out his parish to someone else. His ideal qualities make him ideal to tell the last tale of the trip, a sermon on the Seven Deadly Sins, which reminds us there is a serious spiritual purpose to the pilgrimage and to the *Tales*.

The Plowman

The Parson's brother, in spirit as well as in blood, is the Plowman, who is also the perfect ideal, "living in pees and parfit charite." This portrait may well have amazed Chaucer's audience, just as we'd be surprised to hear of such a chivalrous workman. This Plowman would work for a poor person without pay; he pays all his church taxes on time; he loves his neighbor as himself. He rides a mare, a humble horse. This portrait is especially interesting because peasants in Chaucer's day rose up frequently against Chaucer's own middle class. Some think Chaucer may have presented an ideal plowman because he had such a low opinion of the real ones. But do you think Chaucer would have linked him with the Parson if he meant the picture to be ironic? Even if he is not as rowdy and fully human as some of the others, he is genuine.

The Miller

The Miller certainly is vivid: he's brawny, big-boned, a good wrestler, thick-set. He can rip a door off its hinges. His red beard matches the red bristles that stick out of the wart on his nose. There's no subtle irony here. Chaucer tells us point-blank, "Wel coude he stelen [steal] corn," and charge three times the price. This matches the medieval conception of a miller as the most important, and the most dishonest, tenant on a manor farm. His physical description shows him as shameless, easily angered, and lecherous, according to medieval standards. He leads the group out of town with a bagpipe—which probably has a sexual reference—and uses his big lungs to play it. Later, in his prologue to his raunchy tale about a cuckolded (cheated-on) husband, he cries in "pilate's voice," loud and ranting.

The Manciple

He buys provisions for the "temple," the courts of law, and is shrewd in his buying. Chaucer asks innocently, Isn't it wonderful that such a simple man can outsmart all the learned ones? This idea shows up again and again throughout the *Tales,* with varying results. The Manciple's tale deals with a crow's black feathers (like his own evil ways?) and the necessity for keeping one's mouth shut, which we can therefore assume he is very good at doing!

The Reeve

There's obviously long-standing enmity between the Miller and the Reeve, an official on a farm who would be responsible for keeping tabs on the dishonest Miller. He does well at guarding his lord's seed, poultry, dairy, etc. No one can "bring him in arrerage" (arrears); in fact, sheriffs, shepherds, and workers are scared to death of him—not a sign of goodness in Chaucer's book. The satire is that he gets rich by "lending" his master the master's own money and goods, a common charge against reeves. His description shows him "choleric" in humor, with calfless legs indicating sexual desire. He's trained as a carpenter, which is who the Miller's Tale makes fun of. The fact that he and the Miller ride so far apart, with the Reeve last, shows how badly they get along. We might wonder why they are even on the same pilgrimage. Maybe it's to keep an eye on each other. The Reeve's Tale, to get his own back, is about a miller who tricks a pair of students who then sleep with his wife and daughter.

The Summoner

The Reeve is a model of virtue compared to the Summoner and the Pardoner. Chaucer has saved the worst for last. We can instantly tell that the Summoner is grossly debauched: he has a "fyr-red" face, he is "sawce-fleem" (pimply), and loves garlic, onions, leeks, and wine "red as blood."

NOTE: His skin disease has been shown to be a kind of leprosy, which could come from unclean women or strong foods. Of course, as a church official, he should be avoiding both.

He's stupid, knowing only how to parrot the Latin he's learned from the decrees he hands out. He has all the young girls in the diocese under his control, and is a "good fellow" because he would lend you his mistress for a year for a quart of wine. He can find his own "finch" (quite literally, a chick) in the meantime. The Summoner even wears a "garland," like Bacchus, the god of wine.

He tells good people not to be afraid of the "archdeacon's curse" (excommunication); like a gangster, he can offer "protection" against it if people pay enough. This is a low-down trick that even Chaucer the narrator can't stomach, and he warns that this is the sort of thing that can get you a writ of "significavit" (thrown in jail).

The profession of summoner had reached such depths by Chaucer's day that Chaucer doesn't even need to go into detail on the abuses. A summoner is supposed to deliver a summons to the person charged. But many collected money under the table for extortion and some were even convicted. Not surprising for his personality, the Summoner tells a vulgar tale to get back at the Friar's nasty tale about a summoner. The Summoner tells of a corrupt friar who tricks a rich man and is in turn paid back.

The Pardoner

Pardoners were supposed to issue papal indulgences (forgivenesses of sins) in exchange for alms money, which was to be given to the sick, poor, or another worthy cause. But many pardoners were out-and-out frauds, selling worthless pieces of paper, and even legitimate ones often kept more than their share of the proceeds. This Pardoner is from Rouncivalle, a London hospital well known for the number of illegal pardons connected with it. Most pardoners, like this one, claimed to have come "straight from the court of Rome," with a bagful of pardons "al hoot" off the presses, though of course our Pardoner hasn't set foot outside England.

NOTE: Fake pardoners claimed they could do almost anything for the right sum of money, even remove an excommunication. Despite widespread abuses, though, there still were plenty of people gullible enough to believe in a pardoner's "powers."

There's something suspect in the fact that the Pardoner sings "Come hither, love, to me," to the Summoner, who accompanies him in a strong bass voice.

Some see more than a hint of sexual perversion in this young man who has thin locks of yellow hair that he wears without a hood because he thinks it's the latest style. His small voice and the fact that he has no beard, "ne never sholde [would] have," leads Chaucer to suspect "he were a gelding or a mare"—a eunuch or effeminate man.

NOTE: Scientific opinion of the day believed that thin hair represented poor blood, effeminacy, and deception, while glaring eyes like the Pardoner's indicated folly, gluttony, and drunkenness. Chaucer's audience would catch the references just as we would instantly see the significance of a villain in a black cape and with a black moustache.

As if the description weren't bad enough, the Pardoner tricks people into buying phony relics of saints, such as a pillowcase that he says was "Our Lady's veil," or a piece of sail allegedly belonging to St. Peter. No wonder he makes more money in a day than the poor Parson does in two months. Ironically, Chaucer calls him "a noble eccesiaste," since he can sing a church lesson beautifully—for money, of course. His tale is right in character: he tells what the pilgrims say they want to hear. He says he bases his sermons on money being the root of all evil (he ought to know). But he admits he's not a moral man, although he can tell a moral tale. In his tale about three rowdies, he ironically delivers a sermon against gluttony and other sins. Afterwards, the Host lights into the Pardoner's hypocrisy with such force that the Pardoner is speechless with anger.

The Host

Finally we meet the Host (which is another name for Christ). He is a large man, very masculine (in contrast to the Pardoner), with bright eyes that miss nothing. He's fit to be a "marshall in a hall," a master of ceremonies, which he indeed becomes for the pilgrims. He has the commanding presence to get his plan accepted before it's even told, as long as the pilgrims stand by his judgment—another Christlike reference. The group accepts him as the guide, "governour," judge, and counter of the tales. Tidbits of his personality appear throughout the *Tales*: he's boisterous, well educated, annoyed by his shrewish wife, a jokester, a philosopher; in other words, a full-blooded, complex man. He's a fair leader and promises a free dinner to the best tale-teller, which some see as a moral or parody of a celestial reward. Chaucer carefully mixes religious and worldly references throughout the *Tales*.

Other Elements

SETTING

Setting is more important in some tales than in others. We're told that the Miller's Tale takes place in Oxford, but it could just as well be New Jersey. It's the joke that counts. It's pretty much the same case in the Pardoner's Tale which, because there the moral is important, could take place in England just as easily as Flanders, where the tale is set.

But in the Knight's Tale, the Wife of Bath's Tale, and the Nun's Priest's Tale, settings make moral or ironic points. The Knight's Tale draws connections between the medieval chivalry of England and the society of ancient Greece; the Wife of Bath intentionally places her tale in the days of King Arthur (read her tale and see why); the Nun's Priest's Tale really takes place in a larger setting than a barnyard. You can decide for yourself which settings are important to a tale and why, based on what you think Chaucer is trying to say through the narrator's mouth.

STYLE

As we've already noticed, each tale has a unique personality, which is determined by the character of the tale's narrator. No two are alike. Some are quiet and unassuming, some are loud and carry a punch. Some tales make their point partly through the writing style that Chaucer chooses, such as the Miller's Tale, which is based on a popular raunchy French story form called a *fabliau*. (See the section on "Form and Structure.") Other tales use a different kind of style altogether, like the forthright speaking style of the Wife of Bath.

Yet somehow Chaucer manages to tie them all together in a loose (sometimes even messy) bundle. He does this by contrasting tone of voice, speaker's attitude, and poetic style from tale to tale. We're struck, for instance, by the sharp contrast between the noble and romantic tone of the Knight's Tale and the bawdy parody of knightly language in the Miller's Tale. Of course Chaucer intends this, just as he purposely opposes the characters of the Miller and the Knight (opposites in attitude as well as social standing). The Miller's intent is to show up the Knight and go his tale one better; but in his own way, naturally.

So the way the tale's characters speak to each other in the Miller's Tale will have a bearing on the way we read the tale, whereas in the Wife of Bath's Tale, say, the characters' conversation isn't nearly as important as the point of view that Dame Alice, our loud-mouthed narrator, practically beats over our heads. So, there's a note after the Wife of Bath's Tale that discusses her point of view and attitude as opposed to the Clerk, who tries to answer her back in a tale of his own.

POINT OF VIEW

As you saw just now in the section on "Style," where the Wife of Bath's point of view sneaked in, "style" and "point of view" are closely related in the *Canterbury Tales.* But Chaucer the poet is lurking behind every pilgrim narrator, so that the narrator's point of view isn't the only one.

Chaucer is a remarkably clever writer. He knows exactly how to draw you into each tale so you can see the story, the person telling the story, and the point behind the story (often ironic) all at once. Often Chaucer the poet is making that last point behind the narrator's back, or at the pilgrim's expense, which is what creates the irony.

For example, in the Pardoner's Tale the Pardoner, who is a hypocrite and a sleaze if ever there was one, goes on a moral rampage against drunkenness, lechery, and gluttony—the very sins he's guilty of. Yet the intriguing thing about the tale is not only that you're fascinated by someone so evil, but also that the Pardoner himself is completely unaware (or seems to be) that he's talking about his own damnation. Chaucer is going beyond a potentially boring moralistic tale to show us a real human being, no matter how crass.

As you'll also see, in the note at the end of the Knight's Tale, for example, that point of view sometimes shifts within the tale. When the point of view changes from the Palamon to Arcite and back again, for instance, or from the knights to the arguing gods, decide why you think Chaucer is deliberately changing the scene. Often each point of view represents a different moral or philosophical outlook.

FORM AND STRUCTURE

As with style, Chaucer uses the structure or poetic form of a tale to say something about the narrator or to make a point. The raunchy style of Miller's Tale is inherent in the *fabliau* form, which is by definition a bawdy story. At other times Chaucer contrasts the style of the tale with its form, as in the Wife of Bath's Prologue, which is set in the form of a sermon although her subject matter is hardly sermonlike. The same structural irony occurs in the Pardoner's Tale, where his debauched personality is placed in opposition to his tale's moral structure. Yet in other tales, such as the Nun's Priest's, the overall form of the story isn't as important as its message.

SOURCES

Sometimes Chaucer uses very specific sources for his tales, like the Knight's Tale, and accordingly, notes on sources appear after the discussion of the tale. Others are based more vaguely on general sources like fairy tales (Wife of Bath) or the Bible (the old man in the Pardoner's Tale, perhaps). Still others can't blame their existence on anything but the wonderful genius of Geoffrey Chaucer. As you can tell from this wide a range, the sources for the tales vary greatly, and are sometimes impossible to pin down. But where sources are known, it's interesting to see how Chaucer changed them around.

LANGUAGE

Chaucer is probably the earliest English poet you're likely to read. A first glance at the original Middle English of the *Canterbury Tales*, with all those strange-looking words, might be enough to tempt you to slam the book shut, either in disgust or in terror at having to learn it all. But take a closer look and examine some of the words. You'll see that many aren't any harder to understand than when some people, trying to be "olde"-fashioned, write *shoppe* instead of *shop*. (Chaucer's English is in fact where this idea originated.)

Try to get a dual-language edition of the *Canterbury Tales*, in which the Middle English original is printed on one side of the page and modern English on the other. When you've gotten some practice reading the original words and checking against the modern English, you'll find that the rhythm of Chaucer's poetry gets easier to understand.

Why is it called "Middle English"? Simply because it's at the midpoint between the ancient language spoken by the Anglo-Saxons of England and the English we speak today. In fact, you might feel grateful that you're reading Chaucer instead of the poetry of some of his fellow fourteenth-century poets, because Chaucer's dialect—the Middle English spoken in London—is the language that evolved into our English, while the dialects the other poets used died out. Imagine trying to read something written in a hillbilly drawl or in a Scottish brogue; standard English, even if it's not what we speak all the time, is easier to read.

Even if Chaucer had never written a word, it makes sense that the speech of London, the hub of English society, should develop into the standard English that eventually came over on the *Mayflower*. But Chaucer gave a great boost to the prestige of English, as Shakespeare did later on. It's partly because of Chaucer's terrific (though unintentional) public relations job that the poet John Dryden, three hundred years later, called him "the father of English literature."

There is a robust flavor to Chaucer's language that we can't get in a translation, no matter how good it is. You won't be able to get the nuances of *all* the old words. But after a while you'll almost be able to hear the pilgrims chatting away.

The Tales

GENERAL PROLOGUE: CHARACTERS AND THEMES

The opening of the General Prologue bursts with spring, with new life, and shows that Chaucer is both similar to and different from his poetic predecessors. He uses many images of spring that would be familiar to a medieval audience: the April showers (familiar to us too) "piercing" March's dryness, the "licour" in each plant's "vein," the breezes "inspiring" the crops. It's short, but enough of a description to give us a sense of waking up to new and exciting events. Even the birds sleep with "open eyes" because of the rising sap.

Then, instead of moving from the conventional spring setting to a description of courtly romantic or heroic deeds, as his audience might expect, he draws us into a very down-to-earth world. Spring isn't romance; it's the time of year "when people long to go on pilgrimages." We can all identify with the feeling of "spring fever," when we want to travel and shake off the winter doldrums.

What's more, in case we or Chaucer's listeners are expecting a conventional medieval description of moral allegorical types—Greed, Love, Fortune, etc.—or battles, we're in for a shock. Other poets presented characters for moral purposes or to embody ideals such as courtly love. But Chaucer doesn't deal in types, whether religious or courtly, but in portraits of real people. He even ignores the unwritten rule of the time that, if you're describing someone, you start at the top, very orderly, and work down. Chaucer will start with someone's beard, then hat, boots, tone of voice, and finally his political opinions! (That's just a partial description of the Merchant.) He's not reporting for a moral purpose, but out of love of life and the people around him.

Imagine that you're minding your own business in a wayside tavern and in burst 29 people representing every facet of society. For Chaucer, that meant the nobility, embodied in the Knight and Squire; the church, in the form of the Prioress, Monk, and others; agriculture (the Plowman); and the emerging middle class (the Merchant, Franklin and tradesmen). Rather than shy away from this motley crew, Chaucer the narrator (who is not the same, remember, as Chaucer the poet) befriends and describes them, inserting his own opinions freely.

THE KNIGHT'S TALE

PLOT

Duke Theseus of Athens wins the country of the Amazons and marries Queen Hippolyta, taking her and her beautiful sister Emelye back to Athens. To his amazement, he sees women wailing, but not because of his return. These women have lost their husbands during the siege of Thebes, and Thebes' cruel tyrant Creon refuses to bury the bodies. Theseus immediately vows revenge and rides to Thebes, where he vanquishes Creon and returns their husbands' bones to the women.

In a pile of bodies, pillagers find the young royal Theban knights Palamon and Arcite, who are cousins. They are still alive. Theseus sends them to Athens to be imprisoned for life, and returns home.

Locked in a tower, Palamon one May morning sees Emelye walking in the garden, and falls instantly and madly in love with her. As he explains his love to Arcite, his cousin also spies Emelye and he too is captured by her beauty. Immediately the cousins, who have been as close as brothers since birth, become sworn enemies over the love of Emelye.

Another duke, Perotheus, arrives in Athens to visit Duke Theseus. Perotheus also knows Arcite well, and when he hears the knight is Theseus' prisoner, he begs for Arcite's release. Theseus agrees on condition that Arcite never be seen in any of Theseus' lands, on pain of death. So Arcite returns to Thebes, heartbroken that he can never again see Emelye. At least Palamon, locked in the tower, can look at her, he moans. Meanwhile Palamon sighs that he is wretched, but lucky Arcite can gather an army in Thebes and return to conquer Athens to win the lady.

Finally Arcite can't stand it anymore and risks returning to Athens to see Emelye. He is so pale and thin from lovesickness that he's unrecognizable, so he is able to become a page at Theseus' court, still worshipping Emelye from afar.

One morning Arcite is walking in a grove, exclaiming how unfair it is that he can't even disclose his identity. What he doesn't know is that Palamon has escaped from prison and is overhearing every word from behind a bush. He leaps out and vows to kill Arcite for loving Emelye.

The two agree to meet the next day and fight to the death, but when they do, Theseus, Queen Hippolyta, and Emelye happen along and see the battle. Palamon tells Theseus the whole story, declares his and Arcite's love for Emelye, and admits they both should die for disobeying him. Theseus has pity and declares a tournament joust instead. Each knight may enlist one hundred other knights and whoever wins the battle shall have Emelye.

Palamon prays to Venus, goddess and planet of love. Arcite prays to Mars, god of war. In the heavens, Saturn promises Venus that her favorite, Palamon, shall win. Palamon is captured in the tournament, and Arcite wins. But as Arcite comes forward to accept Emelye, Saturn shakes the ground so that Arcite's horse falls and kills him. As he dies, Arcite asks Emelye to have pity on Palamon if she ever marries.

Years pass, and when mourning for Arcite is over, Theseus declares that the world must go on. He orders Emelye and Palamon to be married, since Palamon has suffered so long for her love. With this happy event, the tale ends.

MAJOR CHARACTERS

Theseus, the wise duke, is firm but fair. We have a picture of him as the strong conqueror, but also as the figure who, like God, dispenses justice along with mercy. For this reason, some have seen Theseus as *the* major character in the Knight's Tale. He personifies the idea of just and reasonable leadership. It's no accident that he rules Athens, the ancient center of learning and reason. He conquers the Amazon nation because it is fitting that a man should be the higher power over women. (This is according to the ideal of knighthood, not necessarily Chaucer's own view. As we shall see, Chaucer pokes fun at some of the courtly conventions even though he greatly admires the Narrator-Knight's behavior.)

Theseus is the representative of order, throughout the tale making a great show of ceremonies and games—such as the joust and the hunting of the hart—that are played by ordered rules.

Arcite believes that Theseus is not really his "mortal enemy," nor is his cousin Palamon. But Arcite is the favorite of Mars, the god of war, so he does not listen to reason.

Instead he follows his own willfullness, which first leads him to go against his cousin, then against his own good fortune. Imagine having your life saved—twice, no less—and cursing your luck because you are set free rather than put to death. We are meant to see Arcite as a man foolish in his willfulness. He is blind to his good fortune: he even complains about men who bemoan fortune's twists, which is exactly what he's doing.

Because of Mars he wins the joust, but he does not realize that fortune is changeable. Only at his death does he begin to see reason and ends the grudge he's been holding for so long against Palamon.

Does **Palamon** get the lady Emelye because he's the better, more valiant knight? He certainly is valiant in the joust—it takes twenty men to capture him—and he is the one who tells Theseus the truth about Arcite's identity and their shared love for Emelye. But where Arcite is overly willful, Palamon refuses to put any stock at all in people's ability to change their situations. He languishes in jail, believing that "man is bounden" to "God's observaunce."

While some readers think that both men are ideal knights from a popular romance, others think Chaucer intended irony in their descriptions, and that indeed neither one of them is worthy of the lady. Or you might think that both are equally worthy, since each has his faults and blind spots yet sincerely upholds what he thinks is right.

What about **Emelye,** the object of affection in all this? For it's hard to see her as much more than an object. Part of the humor of the Knight's Tale comes from the fact that these two knights are pining away over beautiful Emelye for years, while she doesn't yet know they exist. They are ready to kill each other over her, yet we discover that she would rather stay a virgin than marry either one of them.

We may not be quite sure how to take her because we see her only through the eyes of the two knights, who see her in different ways. A hint may be in the way she accepts the dictates of Diana, the goddess of chastity, that she must marry; and so she casts a "freendlich eye" on Arcite when he wins her hand. In general, we're told, women follow "the favour of fortune" *(line 1824)*, as the products of nature do.

STORY LINE

We learn a lot about the Knight's Tale from the very fact that the Knight is chosen to tell the first tale. "Were it by aventure, or sort, or cas" (whether by accident, luck, or chance), the Knight chooses the straw. But it only seems to be random: it's proper that the Knight begin first according to the class structure. So things may appear to be luck when actually there's a plan behind it all.

The Knight will not describe Theseus' feats, he says; then he proceeds to tell us all the things he won't tell us about.

NOTE: This is a device the Knight uses often,
which provides humor and is Chaucer's sly way of
getting in description that is not strictly relevant.

We get a vivid picture of his strength and his love of
"much glory and great solemnity" (pomp). In fact, his
first words show he's annoyed that his homecoming
is marred by women in black crying and upsetting the
order of things.

The first mention of fortune comes from an old
woman who says each of the widows was royalty
before her husband died at Thebes, but now they are
wretches, "Thanked be Fortune and hir false wheel"
(line 67). She adds that fortune doesn't let anyone
remain secure.

Theseus won't stand for this injustice, and he
dashes off to avenge these women. It is women who
throughout the tale will spur him to action and pro-
vide the just ruler with compassion. Here, he's pro-
tective as he pities their plight.

After he has won the battle, Theseus returns to do
"greet honor" to the women, as is orderly and proper.
The burial of the Athenian soldiers is a ritual that
helps man order himself in the universe.

Arcite and Palamon, although of noble birth, are
stuck in a tower until the end of their days. But again,
fortune turns just when you'd think things couldn't
get any worse. Palamon, "by aventure or cas" (another reference to accident or luck), sees Emelye walking
in the garden. She is fresh as nature herself but also
sings as "hevenly" as an angel (line 197). Palamon,
looking at her, can't tell whether she's a woman or a
goddess. But if the two cousins are prisoners, she is

bound, too, by the garden walls, within which she "romed up and doun" *(line 211)*. This is Chaucer's way of showing that fortune circles everyone.

When Palamon cries out as though pierced through the heart, Arcite ironically lectures him on accepting what can't be changed.

> For God's love, endure in patience
> Our prison, for there's no choice;
> Fortune has given us this adversity.
> *(lines 226–228)*

Saturn (the planet that rules chaos), says Arcite, must have given them this misfortune. This is a rational attitude regarding fortune, but it quickly changes when Arcite sees Emelye and falls in love with her himself. Suddenly he is willing to forego his oldest bond of knighthood—his bond with Palamon—for the sake of a lady he has not even met. They start to quarrel, and Palamon accuses Arcite of breaking their sworn oath. Like a child, Palamon claims that Emelye is his because he saw her first.

Arcite notes that there's a difference in each one's love: Palamon loves her in "holinesse," not even knowing whether she's a woman; while Arcite loves her as a fellow "creature" *(lines 300–301)*, that is, as a woman. It may be that Arcite is right, but he uses the argument to prove that "all's fair in love," which justifies breaking his vow. Does it? We'll have to see which vow—love or blood—is the more lasting.

When Arcite's fortune changes through the love of Perotheus and the mercy of Theseus, he's unable to see that it's really God's "purveyaunce" (providence) *(line 394)* that's setting him free. Instead, he can see only as far as the physical things of nature, and moans that not "erthe, water, fyr, ne air/Ne creature" *(lines 388–389)* can help him. (He also uses a classical image of man being "drunk," meaning that his brain is muddled by seeing only lower things and not spiritual heights. But Arcite cannot see that he is doing exactly that.) Palamon's prison, he complains, is really Paradise, and fortune has thrown him good dice *(line 380)*.

Meanwhile Palamon is saying the same things about Arcite. While Arcite wonders why people can't just accept God's will and fortune (which he himself can't), Palamon asks what "governaunce" (justice or reason) there is in God's foreknowledge *(line 455)*. Each knight refuses to accept his fate and is torn between what he wants and what he has, between passion and duty. One is in prison and can see his lady; one is exiled and cut off from his beloved. Which of them, the Knight asks us with a sly grin, is the worse off?

Arcite, pale and ill from love, has a dream in which Mercury, messenger of the gods, tells him,

> To Attenes shaltou wende [go],
> Ther is thee shapen of thy wo an ende
> [there the end of your woe is arranged].
> *(lines 533–534)*

Believing this means he will win Emelye, he risks death by returning to Athens. What he doesn't know is that his "ende" means his death. (In Christian imagery, Mercury often stands for the Devil.)

Fortune takes over from the time that Arcite, "al alone," returns to Athens in disguise.

NOTE: The idea of aloneness versus "company," the ideal of the common good, appears throughout the tale. Theseus, the good ruler, consults his parliament and travels with others. Aloneness, some readers believe, means the way to death.

In a circular pattern, we are back in May, and "Were it
by aventure or destinee (As, when a thing is shapen,
it shal be)" *(lines 607–608)* Palamon escapes just in
time to see Arcite reveal his identity in the grove. Palamon threatens to kill him for breaking their knight's
code and his promise to Theseus not to return. Again,
we are meant to see which promises are the more
important. As we see later, Palamon considers the
knight's honor (which is tied to Venus) to be more
important than winning a battle. Arcite believes the
battle the most important thing.

They agree to fight to the death the next day. Destiny is so strong that it determines what happens, in
this instance and also in all situations—"All is this
ruled by the sight above" *(line 814)*, i.e., God's knowledge. According to the divine plan, Theseus, Hippolyta, and Emelye arrive in the middle of the battle.
Here is where Palamon shows honor by confessing
the whole mess and asking for death.

Theseus is angry that they are fighting "withouten
judge or other officer" *(line 854)*, in other words, outside the order imposed by law and reason. He agrees
to spare their lives when the women plead for mercy
and he sees that the fight is over love. He is still angry
in his heart, "Yet in his reason he them both excused"
(line 908).

Theseus decides to settle the problem in an ordered
game of battle where no one will be killed. This battle
will determine whether love or might triumphs.

Part III opens with a lavish description of Theseus'
building of the joust arena and the altars prepared for
the gods of the main characters: Venus for Palamon,
Mars for Arcite, Diana for Emelye. Each god is depict-
ed in the cruelest terms—Venus as the goddess of

lovers' "broken sleeps" and "cold sighs" *(line 1062)*; Mars as the war god that brings death and destruction; Diana, goddess of chastity, as a cruel huntress.

Each knight prays for victory and gets a sign that he interprets as meaning that he'll be victorious. At the same time, the gods argue it out in the heavens, with Saturn, the god and planet of death, promising Venus that her man Palamon will win eventually. But she and Mars must keep peace between them for awhile, since their opposition creates "swich divisioun" *(line 1618)*.

Even though Saturn is a mean spirit, his main purpose here is to create harmony among the gods and the mortals below. Life can't exist without harmony or without pain, Saturn is saying; the suggestion is that this is the reason behind fortune's ups and down.

The final section takes us onto the battlefield where Arcite's knights fight for Mars (and Emelye) and Palamon's for Venus (and Emelye). The rhetorical description of the battle, which some say represents sexual struggle, embodies human conflict the way cowboy films do; knights fall off horses and the crowd cheers or boos. Finally Mars' knight Arcite wins the contest.

When Arcite's short-lived victory is literally overturned by his pitching horse, we're told that the "expulsive," "animal," or "natural" virtues couldn't help him.

NOTE: Three virtues, the vital, natural, and animal, were believed to control the body. In Arcite, the animal virtue, connected with the brain, can't expel the poison from the natural virtue, connected with the liver. "Nature" loses her hold on his life.

He dies "Allone, withouten any company," without having gained the desire of his dreams.

The only consolation for Arcite's death comes from Theseus' old father Egeus, who knows "the world's transmutation" and has seen it change "both up and down" *(lines 1981–1982)*. This reminds us of love as well as life, for we've been told before that lovers go "now up, now down, like a bucket in a well" *(line 675)*. The world always changes according to fortune, Egeus says, and he reminds us of the wider context of the tale when he says

> This world is just a thoroughfare of woe,
> And we are pilgrims, passing to and fro.
> *(lines 1989–1990)*

There is even some humor in the orderly telling of Arcite's funeral, which the Knight describes by saying what he won't describe. But after this ritual of death and honor, life begins again with Theseus explaining the point of the tale, that life's order is a natural one, of fortune, love, life, and death. Everything is part of a perfect whole established by the First Mover (God), but lives its allotted time before the next generation succeeds.

> Then it is wisdom, as it seems to me,
> To make a virtue of necessity. . . .
> *(lines 2183–2184)*

In other words, Theseus makes the best of the nature we are given. Pain and death are inevitable, but let's enjoy it all to get the most out of life. What Palamon and Arcite couldn't settle between them—the problems of passion, duty, and fortune—are resolved by Theseus in this wise speech.

The marriage of Palamon and Emelye is the outcome of this philosophy, and also shows how, within the wheel of fortune, happiness can exist along with, even because of, sadness and suffering.

SOURCE

Chaucer takes the tale of Palamon and Arcite from Boccaccio's *Teseide*, which basically tells the same story but which is, believe it or not, five times longer than Chaucer's version. He condenses the first book and a half of Boccaccio's work into the first few lines of the Knight's Tale, saying the story is long enough without the detail of Theseus' battle with the Amazons.

The original has Egeus' words of comfort in Theseus' mouth; Chaucer changes it so he could give the grand ending speech to the duke. The speech itself—in fact, the whole idea of fortune's wheel—comes from Boethius, an early Christian philosopher, whom Chaucer translated into English and whose philosophy infects many of the tales. Evidently Chaucer liked the idea of wheels within wheels; fortune causes rises and falls in the world, while above it all God's providence remains stable.

SETTING

Of course the story is supposed to be taking place in ancient Greece, but that doesn't stop Chaucer from giving one of the jousting knights a Prussian (German) shield, for example, or holding a joust (a medieval game) in the first place. But Chaucer obviously thinks people are people, whether they're in ancient Greece or medieval England, and that's the major difference between his rendition of Boccaccio's tale and the original. For all the stylized descriptions and conventions, he's giving us people with conflicts who are not perfect.

THEMES

1. WHO ARE THE GODS?

Fortune, as we have seen, plays a large part in the tale. The gods act as agents of that fortune at the same time that they represent the order of God. ("Jupiter" is named as the First Mover, God, since after all this is supposed to be pre-Christian Greece.)

How, you might ask, can it be a poem about God's plan if there are pagan gods running the show? Chaucer gets out of this potentially sticky problem brilliantly by subtly changing the gods to their respective planets. They still talk and act like gods, but the influence they exert is in the form of astrological influences, which many in Chaucer's audience would accept. It's not Saturn the cruel god who topples Arcite from his horse, it's the influence of Saturn an evil planet. The gods/planets also embody abstract ideals, Venus representing both good and bad love, Diana showing cruel as well as proper chastity.

2. SOCIAL ORDER

An ordered society represented by ceremony and ritual is crucial to a smoothly running world. Theseus also shows this by conquering the Amazon society, run by women, and Creon, who is not ruled by reason. Another symbol of the importance of society is the stress on "compaignye," which is the opposite of death where man is alone, as Arcite bewails in his dying speech. The marriage ending shows the ultimate victory of the social world over the solitary one.

3. VOWS

Arcite and Palamon break their vow of kinship and knighthood; they vow faithfulness to the gods of their choice; they vow undying love for Emelye. These promises made and broken show the conflict of ideals and the difficulty of keeping them, because of fortune's turns and humanity's nature. The only one who's different is Theseus, who changes his mind only when he tempers his vows with mercy. You must look at the two knights' vows and determine which ones are the most important to keep.

4. FORTUNE

The wheel of fortune image was very familiar to Chaucer's audience. The wheel of fortune spins, making paupers kings, and vice versa, but behind it is the stable, unchanging providence of God, which we can't see or understand. So there are two levels of understanding, one in which men blame fortune for their ever-changing lives, and a higher order where destiny is decreed. Arcite lives on the lower level and believes fortune rules everything, while Palamon accepts that whatever is ordained will happen.

POINT OF VIEW

Chaucer brings us closer to the Knight's Tale by occasionally switching into an "I" narration, such as when he describes the altars Theseus has built to Mars:

> There saw I first the dark imagining
> Of Felony, and all the compassing [planning]
> > *(lines 1137-1138)*

He also changes his point of view from telling of first one person, then another; from telling of human exploits to the arguments of the gods. This makes us feel like we ourselves are gods, able to see more than any individual character.

FORM AND STRUCTURE

Some believe the Knight's Tale is a pure romance, filled with knights and lovely ladies and battles for the sake of love. At several points it's clear Chaucer is making fun of the courtly love conventions of the French romances, with the lovesick Arcite going "up and down" in his moods. Duke Theseus, too, treats the love battle like a game, making light of love and offering the joust as a solution.

Others think the tale, which Chaucer changed greatly from Boccaccio's original, starts out as an epic before it becomes a conventional romance in its style. Another irony is that Theseus' speech at the end would not have appeared in a conventional romance tale.

THE MILLER'S TALE

PLOT

The Miller's Tale is not supposed to follow the Knight's Tale, for the Monk, who is next to the Knight in the social order, should go next. But the drunken Miller cuts in, insisting that he will tell a tale first or else leave the group. The Reeve tells him to shut up, but the Miller insists.

A well-meaning but stupid carpenter named John has a lodger, a poor scholar named Nicholas. Nicholas buries himself in astrology books, likes to play music and mess around with women, and lives off his friends. John, meanwhile, has a young wife, only eighteen, named Alison, of whom he's extremely jealous.

Not surprisingly, Nicholas starts to make a pass at Alison one day while John is away. She protests only a little before agreeing that if Nicholas can find a way to keep John from finding out, she'll sleep with him. Don't worry, says Nicholas, a clerk can surely fool a carpenter.

Meanwhile, a parish clerk named Absalom, who is as particular as Nicholas about his appearance and his appeal to women, sees Alison at church and decides to woo her. He sings under the bedroom window that night, waking up John in the bargain. He tries everything he can think of, but Alison is so infatuated with Nicholas that she pays no attention.

Nicholas comes up with a plan that will let him and Alison spend all night together. He stays in his room for days, until John gets worried and breaks down the door.

Nicholas warns him, in confidence, that he has seen a terrible omen in his astrology books. There will be a flood that will make Noah's flood look like a drizzle. In order to be saved, Nicholas tells John that he must get three large tubs and hang them from the roof until the flood reaches that high; then they can cut the ropes and float away.

But you must not sleep with your wife that night, Nicholas warns, because there must be no sin between you.

Gullible John believes every word. On the appointed night he strings up the boats and falls asleep in one of them. Needless to say, Nicholas and Alison live it up.

But Absalom, having heard that John is out of town, hightails it to the house and stands under the window again, begging for a kiss. As a joke, Alison agrees, and under cover of night she sticks her rear end out the window for Absalom to kiss.

He gets furious and his love for Alison evaporates. He runs to a blacksmith and takes a hot iron back to the house, calling to Alison that he wants to give her a gold ring. This time Nicholas decides to put his rear end out the window to be kissed.

"Speak, dear," says Absalom, since it's too dark to see. Nicholas farts.

He gets a hot poker where it hurts, and shrieks, "Help! Water!" The cry wakes up John, who thinks the cry of "Water!" means the flood has begun. He cuts the rope and crashes to the ground, fainting and breaking his arm in the process. The tale ends with John the laughingstock of the town, Nicholas amply repaid for his deceit, and Alison having gotten the "plumbing" she desired.

MAJOR CHARACTERS

Nicholas is the sliest character in Chaucerian literature. He is "hende," a word that means "nice" and "pleasant," but also carries hints of "sly" and "handy," in other words, ready for action. He knows all about love, sexual pursuits, and astrology. He's amazingly creative, devising a complicated scheme to sleep with Alison and to make John believe his wild story.

NOTE: Chaucer's emphasis on the creativity of rogues in his tales is something brand new to the Middle Ages. Before this it was unheard of to grant anything like cunning to any evil character except the Devil himself.

Chaucer's audience would recognize his name from plays about St. Nicholas, who is the mysterious guest at the home of evil hosts. Here, it's the other way around.

Alison is charming. Some think she's not terribly
bright, while others see Chaucer's portrait of her as a
wholehearted endorsement of youth. Her description
is filled with animal and nature images: her body is
graceful as a weasel's, she's softer than sheep's wool,
and better to look at than a pear tree. (Remember this
image. In the Merchant's Tale the pear tree becomes a
symbol of adultery.) She's skittish as a colt, and the
apron around her loins is white as morning milk. That
sounds sweet and pure, but her eyes are wanton
under her plucked eyebrows. The Miller calls her by
flowers' names—a primrose and a "piggesnye,"
which also means "pig's eye." So the suggestion of
pastoral innocence is offset by a sense of natural
instincts and unthinking passion.

Absalom is a real dandy, as anxious as Nicholas to
hop into bed with pretty women. But where Nicholas
is a man of action, taking what he wants, Absalom
does things the polite way, singing songs under Alison's window and following proper ceremony. He's
immensely particular about his appearance and his
scent, which could explain why he's squeamish about
farting.

Chaucer's description is more appropriate to a
romance heroine than to a man, with his prettily
curled hair and rosy complexion. He's not "hende"
like Nicholas, he's "jolly," which could explain why
he's useless in getting anywhere with Alison. Because
he's so exact about his clothes, some see him as a
typical small-town lover boy, without intelligence. But
he's not unlikable. When you're in love, it's sometimes hard to think of anything but the object of your
desire.

John is someone we don't really see, in the sense
that he's not physically described. There's a reason for
this: he stays in the background while Nicholas, Ali-

son, and Absalom fill the stage. Yet John, even
though he's stupid, is a nice guy. He's truly concerned about Nicholas when the schemer is in his
"fit," and his first thought is for Alison when he hears
the end of the world is at hand. Significantly, his
name reminds us of St. John, whose gospel describes
the next "flood," or Doomsday. The irony to Chaucer
is that the carpenter's knowledge is not true, as
opposed to the knowledge revealed in the Bible.

STORY LINE

After the Knight's Tale, the Host remarks, "unbo-
keled is the male" *(line 7)*, meaning the pouch contain-
ing the tales is unbuckled, but also meaning a man's
pants are undone. This sets us up for the crudeness of
the drunken Miller's tale, in which double meanings
abound.

The Miller promises a tale to get back at the
Knight.

NOTE: This isn't a personal rivalry, like the Miller's with the Reeve, but reminds us that the tales
work on two levels: presenting different points of
view from tale to tale on various issues, and setting
the actual pilgrims against one another.

The Miller also lets on he'll parody religious themes
by saying he will tell "a legende and a life" *(line 33)*,
which usually means a life of the saints. But this one's
about a "clerk" (scholar) who makes a fool of a carpenter. This infuriates the Reeve, a carpenter by
trade.

The "Chaucer" who's narrating the pilgrimage apologizes for repeating the Miller's vulgarity, but emphasizes he has to repeat what he hears. If you want, you can turn to another tale that's more morally uplifting. But whatever your choice, don't blame him!

Right off we're told that the carpenter is a rich scoundrel, and a poor scholar lives under his roof. This leads us instantly to be sympathetic to the scholar. He knows so much about astrology that he can predict when it will rain (it is this talent that later makes John believe him), and also, like a joke on God, knows what the future will bring. Nicholas knows about love that is "derne"—discreet and private, but also meaning secret and sinful. He looks meek as a maid, but appearances are deceiving, an important point to keep in mind.

The old carpenter, who doesn't know he should marry someone his own age, has a young wife because he fell into the "snare" of love. This will cause him trouble, as we shall see.

Alison is compared to a gold coin, a valuable piece of material goods, but she is vividly human. We even know how far up her legs her shoes are laced. She's "noble" (a kind of gold coin), fit for a lord, and also fit for a yeoman (servant). This prepares us for the humorous contrast throughout the tale of the courtly with the common.

NOTE: There is also a contrast between this and the preceding Knight's Tale. Both deal with two men after the same woman, and both concern the issues of love and what is beyond man's control, though on very different levels.

When Nicholas makes a bold pass at Alison, the sexual references come hot and heavy. He grabs her "queynte" (lines 89–90), which can mean strange, or sly, or a woman's genitals (here it's used in the last two senses). He must have her or he will "spille" (die or ejaculate). He adds that his plan will work because a clerk can fool a carpenter any day. This class distinction is humorous in the circumstances, since all the characters are common even though they're trying to be noble and courtly.

Right after planning adultery, Alison is off to church, juxtaposing the profane and the sacred in a way some might find sacrilegious. By the same token, "jolly" Absalom shouldn't, as a parish clerk, be hanging out in every tavern in town. He goes to church to check out the wives, Alison among them.

He falls for her, offering her things as befits the conventions of courtly love. But there is an undercurrent of foolishness and lechery: instead of rich gifts, he woos Alison with pies and ale, and he offers a bribe. He even plays Herod as in a mystery play, a role that involves exaggerated language and contortions. But Alison prefers Nicholas.

When Nicholas disappears for two days, John gets genuinely worried. When he discovers Nicholas' "fit," John says it's not men's business to know about God's "privetee" (secret affairs), a word that will appear again, in reference not to God but to the affair of Alison and Nicholas.

John tells Nicholas to "look down" (line 291), i.e., away from God's business, and think about Christ's passion instead. But the silly carpenter then falls for Nicholas' scheme, believing that Nicholas is indeed as knowledgeable as God. He's put his money on the wrong spiritual horse. Nicholas says he won't tell "God's privetee" (again, an ironic usage), as if he knows what God's plans really are.

Hypocritically, Nicholas tells John that he and Alison must not sleep together because they will be awaiting God's grace. The joke here is that Nicholas doesn't realize that God sent Noah the flood because man had become corrupt and lecherous. The same sins are causing this phony "flood," even though the plan this time isn't God's.

John tells Alison *his* "privetee" (secret), although of course Alison knows exactly what the "queynte" plan is, in both senses of the word. She tells John she is his faithful wife—another word that John accepts as Gospel—and John follows Nicholas' instructions and makes the preparations, just as Noah obeyed God even though everyone laughed at him.

Alison and Nicholas have a merry time of it until the morning church bells ring. The reference to the couple's sex in the same breath as the church is meant to shock, and to show that man's plans often unintentionally mirror God's order.

Absalom goes to the house, believing Alison is alone, and performs a parody of a morning prayer, asking for Alison's grace and mercy instead of God's. The "kiss" she gives him brings him down to earth in a hurry. His love is "all y-queynt," all quenched, but again this is a pun. Like someone in the Old Testament, he vows revenge. It's interesting that he chooses to come back with a hot "colter" (a plowshare), a backward use of the Biblical adage about turning swords into plowshares.

Nicholas gets what he deserves. And Absalom, because he is "squeamish of farting," gets what he deserves also, for wishing for something he shouldn't have. And their whole world comes crashing down with John when Nicholas cries for water to cool his burned behind. Justice is served and God's order is reestablished at the expense of a lower kind of plan.

SOURCE AND STRUCTURE

There's no source for the amazing complications of the Miller's Tale except Chaucer's own amazing mind. However, the idea of a woman sticking her backside out a window for an unwanted lover to kiss comes from a raucous Middle English song called "Old Hogan's Adventure."

The form of the tale is the French *fabliaux*, earthy folktales that involve a wife cheating on her husband. (The church disapproved of such tales, which probably was one reason why they were so popular.) This kind of tale joins profane elements with references to sacred teachings, but Chaucer combines them so successfully that they're almost impossible to separate.

LANGUAGE

One of the best jokes in Chaucer's funniest tale is the way the characters use the language of courtly love to gain their selfish, lustful ends. Nicholas and Absalom call Alison "lemman," sweetheart, and Alison speaks of Nicholas' "courtesy," which we certainly don't take seriously. This is a humorous contrast to the seriousness of love in the Knight's Tale, and also reminds us that the ultimate purpose of courtly love, no matter how noble it sounded, was sexual conquest.

THEMES

1. NOAH AND THE FLOOD

In the Bible, Noah saves the best left on earth when God sends the flood to destroy the world for its corruption. Typically Noah was seen in the Middle Ages as the precursor to Christ, who also saves. By referring to the Noah story, Chaucer uses the idea of man following God's plan, even though he doesn't know what the plan is.

2. DESTINY AND IDEAS OF ORDER

There's a right way and a wrong way to do things, as we learned in the Knight's Tale, to which this tale is an answer and a parallel. The earlier tale deals with destiny that men can't change or know about; here it takes the form of everyone getting his or her just deserts. All the individual plans backfire and God's proper order is reestablished.

Also, we're meant to see, even in this humorous tale, that some things belong to a natural order: men should marry women their own age, young people will be attracted to each other and let their sexual instinct override their sense.

3. VOCATIONS

Everyone's profession has an ironic meaning in this tale. Carpentry, John's profession, is put in to annoy the Reeve, but look at it also in a larger sense. Carpentry was Christ's profession. Also, the carpenter's guild in Chaucer's day put on the mystery (religious) play of Noah. Astrology is what allows Nicholas to pull one over on John. But it also was seen by some in the Middle Ages as a "wrong" science, since man's "privetee" and providence aren't supposed to replace God's, and astrology is a way to try to do so. Like

Arcite in the Knight's Tale, Nicholas is set apart from society; he is set apart by his dabbling in the occult.

4. PROMISES

As in the Knight's Tale, vows are made and broken, but the humor here is that half the time the people who make the promises don't intend to keep them. Alison is not the faithful wife. Nicholas promises a flood that never comes. The only promises that are kept are the wrongly intentioned ones, such as Alison and Nicholas' vow to cuckold John, Nicholas' promise to John that he will "save" his wife, and Alison's promise that she'll let Absalom kiss her.

5. THE SACRED AND PROFANE

We've already seen the interplay between the bawdy and the religious, but how are we to take it? Does the profanity cast doubt on the seriousness of the spiritual? Does the idea of a hidden moral mean we can't take the tale's raucousness at face value? You can accept either version, or make a case that Chaucer meant to fuse the two, with the lovers' longings and the love of God represented. After all, you can argue in this tale that both sex and religion are ways to reach outside of oneself, and both come in for their fair share of ridicule.

✓ THE WIFE OF BATH'S TALE
PLOT

Unique in the Canterbury Tales, the introduction to The Wife of Bath's Tale is longer than the tale itself. She describes her views on marriage in great detail, starting with the grief she's given all five of her husbands (and which she had a great time dishing out).

Her purpose in marriage has been to gain the upper hand. Her first three husbands were old, rich, and willing to do what she said. She used harangues to get them on the defensive when they got suspicious of her stepping out, accusing them of looking at other women.

Her fourth husband had a mistress, but Dame Alice (the Wife) made him fry in his own grease. She had him believe she was sleeping with another man (she wasn't) so he'd be jealous. But even before he died Alice started making eyes at a clerk, Jankin, while Husband #4 was in London during Lent. When the fourth husband died, Alice married the good-looking Jankin, twenty years her junior: the only one she married for love and the only one who treated her like dirt.

He used to read to her from a book that told how women can't be trusted. She got so furious that she ripped the pages out, and he hit her so hard she went partially deaf. Thinking (or at least making him think) she was about to die, she made him swear to obey her every word. After that, they had a perfect marriage.

Before the Wife begins her tale, the Friar butts in and the Summoner yells at him. (They are natural enemies because they both try to get money from people.) Because he has interrupted, the Wife starts her story with an attack on friars' lechery.

Her tale, not surprisingly, exemplifies the same theme. A knight is sentenced to death for raping a woman, but the queen will allow him to live if he can answer one question: what do women want? He finds no two people who agree, until an old woman tells him women want mastery in marriage. Because she gives him the right answer, he must grant her request, which is that he marry her.

He's horrified but has no choice. On their wedding night, she offers to stay ugly and faithful, or turn young and beautiful and perhaps unfaithful. Wisely, he leaves the choice up to her and promises her domination over him. So she becomes beautiful *and* faithful and they live happily. The Wife ends by praying God to send every woman a young, sexy, and obedient husband!

MAJOR CHARACTERS

Dame Alice, the Wife herself, is her own main character. She gives us a vivid picture of herself. Obviously she loves to talk and pauses only when she's lost her place in her long ramble. She tells us *(lines 609–616)* that she was born when Venus and Mars were in conjunction with Taurus. According to this horoscope, Venus would make her beautiful, but Mars would make her heavy. The sweet voice bestowed by Venus becomes loud and raucous thanks to Mars' planetary influence. All in all, the planets make her charming, joyous, and boisterous.

Some readers say Dame Alice is totally lifelike, others say she is larger than life. Some say she loves men, as they are obviously her life-long passion, while others contend she is carrying on a life-long war against them. You decide. Is she at fault for wanting dominion over her husbands? (Your answer should depend on what you see in the character, not on whether you're male or female.) Notice that she not only puts men down, she also satirizes women, pointing out that they can't keep their mouths shut and that she's right up there with the worst of them.

Another question is how she feels about the life she's lived. When she stops to think of her vanished youth, you can see it as a real sadness over lost time, or as a shrug of her shoulders and a joyous desire to get on with the rest of her life. Either way, Chaucer doesn't praise or blame her, but lets her look forward to her sixth husband, whoever he may be.

The **Knight** in the tale is not well defined, because he's more of a receptacle for Dame Alice's teachings than a man in his own right. Because he rapes a woman (a virgin, at that) he's sentenced to death; but we don't hear a peep from him. In fact, the only time we see any emotion on his part is when he's upset: at discovering he has an impossible task to perform, at hearing that he has to marry the old hag, at having to sleep with her. The only time he is genuinely happy, in fact, is when the wife has total control over him (and has become young and faithful). This is the point Dame Alice wants to convey.

The **Old Woman** in the tale doesn't have a name, but she packs a powerful moral punch. When the knight complains in bed about having to sleep with a wife who is old, poor, and ugly, she delivers a strong and well-reasoned sermon about the nobility that comes from God, not from a bloodline. Finally she shows she will win his love by becoming both beautiful and faithful. Her intelligence and reasoned responses are as articulate as those of the Wife herself.

STORY LINE

Introduction

Dame Alice tells us straight off that experience is the only authority she needs to tell of the problems of marriage. She proceeds, however, to use plenty of other authorities to support her idea that women should have control in marriage.

NOTE: ⭑ In the Middle Ages women had an exceptionally raw deal in marriage. Legally, they could do nothing without their husbands, in fact did not even exist other than as their husbands' property. Even sex could technically be performed only for procreation, not enjoyment (that was lust). Look at the effect this attitude has, not only on the way a medieval audience would view this tale, but the Miller's Tale as well. Women were responsible for any lust a man felt, because they were all considered temptresses.

Immediately Dame Alice gets defensive about the number of husbands she's had, saying not even Christ himself defined how many husbands were too many.

She first lets us know that virginity is nothing worth defending, since although St. Paul advises virginity, he doesn't command it; he leaves it up to each woman. There's no prize for virginity, she says in her own defense; besides, she cleverly asks, if everyone were a virgin, where would we get virgins?

Everyone has a gift from God, and uses it as best he or she can. This is a defense for her own healthy sexual appetite that flies in the face of the prevailing attitude. This attitude is upside-down from an orthodox medieval viewpoint: rather than trying to understand men's (and women's) actions according to a divine plan, she deduces God's plan for the world according to earthly desires and needs. But, she says, God wouldn't have made sexual organs if not for pleasure. (You can still hear this same argument today.) At least she is willing to have sex, unlike other wives who are "daungerous" (cool and standoffish).

Given the attitude of the time, is it outrageous of her to want to have a husband who will be her debtor and slave and to have power over his body *(lines 155-*

158)? After all, that's the legal power a husband can hold over her. She uses authors to support her case, but adds she's saying all this only to amuse the company.

Believing that the best defense is a good offense, she teaches how to accuse husbands of being in the wrong to make them mind. All she wants to do, she pretends, is please them. At the same time, they're old, so why should they want her sex all to themselves when there's plenty to go around?

NOTE: This is an ironic upset of the idea of mutual charity in marriage, and of the assumption that men and women of the same age should marry. This may be valid, as the three old husbands died trying to satisfy her.

She thumbs her nose at the medieval wisdom that says a woman's love is like a fire—the more it burns the more it wants to burn. But without her false accusations against her former husbands, she'd be ruined—"Been spilt," a sexual allusion as it is with Nicholas in the Miller's Tale—if she didn't take the initiative. She sees marriage in a cold, practical light: first come, first served; and whoever can profit should do so, for everything in life is for sale. She doesn't have sexual feeling for the old husbands, but pretends to so she can get things from them. Is this a cruel and callous attitude or is Dame Alice getting her just deserts?

Dame Alice's fourth husband, even though he was a lout (pulling off the very cheating tricks she accused the other husbands of), makes her think fondly of her lost youth. But the passing of time doesn't cause her to regret the good times she's had. Time has robbed her of her beauty, but "the devil with it" *(line 476)*. Her resigned observation that "the flour is gone," meaning both "flour" and "flower," is ambiguous, showing her deep-rooted sense of the flesh and her sense of lost youth.

She loved her last two husbands because they were cool toward her. There's no real change or growth in her more recent experience, but these husbands, especially the last, are more like her and so more successful as matches. They give her a dose of her own medicine, and even though she eventually gets control, she gets a good fight in the process.

Jankin is the only husband we get a clear picture of, as well as the circumstances surrounding their meeting and wooing. It gives us a clue as to how she may have arranged her other marriages. (Like Nicholas, he is "hende," and she, like Alison, feels an instant sexual attraction.) We can feel Dame Alice's frustration after hearing of the tales of evil women that Jankin reads her, of the man who wants a cutting of the "blessed tree" on which a man's three wives hanged themselves and the proverbs that prove all wives are wicked.

The ending is a happy one for her, for although she uses trickery, pretending she's about to die, she does get her "mastery," which means skill as well as superiority. In this success, has she reached beyond the instinctual knowledge she's depended on all these years? Her tale may indicate an answer.

The Tale

Dame Alice's nasty reference to "limiters" (friars who beg within certain limits) to get back at the Friar's comment on her big mouth, shows in what disrepute friars are viewed: a woman is safe, she says, since the friar will take only her honor. This is a nice lead-in to the main tale, where a knight does indeed take a young woman's honor.

The knight sees women only as objects that he can take by force. But ironically his life then depends on the will of women.

NOTE: As in the Knight's Tale, mercy is dependent on the goodness of women. Pity, whether between the sexes, ruler and subject, or God and man, is another form of love.

Dame Alice jokes at her own expense about women who want to be free instead of listening to their husbands, and about women who, like Midas' wife (and like herself), can't keep their mouths shut.

The knight learns that women want many things, but most of all they want dominion over their men, an assertion of identity just as men have. The old woman from whom he learns this is obviously enchanted, for the 24 dancing women in the forest disappear, and she knows, without being told, that he's been sent by the queen.

The knight has more to learn after he's forced to marry the old woman. His idea of the natural order makes it abhorrent to think of marrying someone so old and below his station, but he is to be morally reeducated, appropriately, in bed.

Her arguments—that "gentilesse" (nobility) comes from God, that poverty can be a blessing, and that ugliness keeps a woman faithful—are based on authorities like Christ and Dante. This shows a strong Christian basis for her position, a basis Jankin was missing when he quoted from his learned book. They make sense, but neither choice (faithful but ugly or beautiful and faithless) holds water against the strength of human nature. He has to choose between physical and spiritual love, and he chooses neither. Both choices involve dilemmas: possession without joy or independence with jealousy.

By resigning himself, the knight shows true repentance and spiritual growth, and he is rewarded by getting the impossible, youth and fidelity. But first he has to relinquish control, a fact that echoes Dame Alice's own marriage to Jankin. The balance reached in the end is based on a harmony between sexuality and spiritual values, and even if Dame Alice doesn't have quite the same balance in her marriage, she at least has put her point across in a lively and convincing way.

SOURCES

Dame Alice's tale is a satire put in the form of a fairy tale. She is twisting an old folk tale that shows up in an Arthurian romance about Sir Gawain, one of Arthur's knights. In that story the choice is between a wife who is beautiful either by day or by night—a very different kind of choice from the one our knight is offered.

The tale serves as an "exemplum," a moral tale that preachers used to show people how they should act. For similar reasons, her introduction, complete with authorities and logical arguments, is in the form of a university sermon so she can persuasively make her case for pleasurable sex that goes against medieval doctrine. Many of the antifeminist points are taken from St. Jerome, notably the image of woman's love burning like a fire and seeking more to burn. Of course, in Dame Alice's mouth the idea of putting sexual guilt on the woman sounds ridiculous.

The Wife herself is based loosely on the Old Woman in the French *Romance of the Rose*, which Chaucer translated. Like Alice, the Old Woman has used love for sensual pleasure and gain, and defends the philosophy against courtly love or Scripture. But the source is more in the Old Woman's ideas than her person, since she's old and decrepit and Dame Alice still has plenty of years—and husbands—left to go.

SETTING

It's appropriate that Dame Alice would choose the mythical, misty time of King Arthur's Round Table for her tale. It's a time of chivalry and enchantment. By placing her tale beyond a specific time, in a place where the woman's love was the all-important factor in a knight's courtly conduct, she's making sure her audience will catch the importance of female superiority.

THEMES

1. SEXUAL SUPERIORITY

Some read the Wife of Bath's whole saga as one of sexual revenge, but consider the society she has to put up with. Restrictions on women were enormous in Chaucer's day, and Dame Alice wants to gain revenge inside marriage. Her feminism was perhaps not common, but protests like hers weren't unheard of either. She means to attack the guilt-ridden and sex-obsessed attitudes of her day by beating men at their own game.

2. CELIBACY/VIRGINITY

Although she quotes St. Paul on the sanctity of virginity, Dame Alice isn't ashamed of the fact that she wants no part of it. Her rambunctious sexuality is in itself a kind of religious devotion, since it glorifies God by making good use of the tools He gave her.

3. AUTHORITY

Dame Alice uses her obvious intelligence in defense of the carnal, but she also pulls in as many authorities on the subject as she can think of, both for her introduction and the old hag's speech. Many of her "quotations" from learned men are loose translations indeed, or outright misunderstandings, for example when she freely translates St. Paul's teachings on chastity. Yet, as she begins by saying, her greatest authority is her own experience.

4. CHOICE

The knight must choose between appearances and satisfaction, between a good-looking wife or a faithful one. Dame Alice too makes it clear that she has chosen her five husbands, rather than them choosing her, though she's not particular. It all boils down to her idea of being in control of one's own life, which she identifies as superiority in marriage.

5. KINDS OF LOVE

Of course, the most important kind is sexual, but as the example of the queen shows, there is also the noble love called pity; the love, warring or peaceful, between husband and wife; and the love that Christ (whom Dame Alice likens to a woman because he was a virgin) has for humanity. The different kinds of love are intertwined for her because they are all part of the constantly changing facets of love that make up a marriage.

POINT OF VIEW

Dame Alice is loud and direct in supporting her point of view that sex is meant for pleasure and women are to carry the big stick in marriage. This lusty viewpoint gives us a clear idea of her attitudes and priorities.

But not everyone agrees. Later on, the Clerk gives a tale back, measure for measure, that is exactly the opposite of Dame Alice's.

THE PARDONER'S TALE
PLOT

The Pardoner, like the Wife of Bath, begins his tale with a long introduction that shows us remarkable things about his character. He freely admits he uses the same tricks every place he goes, with the same sermon—"Love of money is the root of all evil." He shows people his credentials, then the animal bones he passes off as holy relics, which he lies can cure sick animals, increase livestock, even cure jealousy. He makes 100 marks a year by preaching against greed, shaming people into parting with their money. But he does this only out of his own covetousness, not to help people. *He* won't live in poverty, that's for sure. Even though he knows he's completely unscrupulous, he can still tell a moral tale.

The Pardoner sets up the pilgrims the same way he does his gullible parishioners. First he rails against drunkenness, gluttony, gambling, and swearing. Then he tells the warning tale of three young men of Flanders (Belgium) who are guilty of all these things.

While they're drinking in a bar, a dead body goes by. It happens to be a friend of theirs. A servant boy tells them Death is the culprit who is going around killing everyone. (It's during a plague.) The three rioters decide—drunkenly—to go find this Death and kill him.

They meet an old man who is covered except for his head. He is polite, but the three young men are rude to him. The old man wants to die, but can't find anyone who will trade his youth for the old man's age. Thinking he's Death's spy, the rioters make him tell where Death is. The man points to a large tree, saying they'll find Death underneath it.

But what they find is eight bushes of florins (gold coins), and, delighted, decide to wait until night to move them. They send the youngest rogue into town to buy wine, and while he's gone, the other two decide to stab the third when he returns, so they can split the gold. The youngest, meanwhile, has the same idea and poisons the wine in order to kill the other two.

Everything goes as planned—all three ending up dying. Alas, cries the Pardoner, look what comes from gluttony and pride! And he offers pardons for redemption, although he admits that Christ's pardon is better than his.

In an epilogue to his tale, the Pardoner actually tries to palm off some of his "relics" on his fellow pilgrims, starting with the Host, whom he calls the most sinful of the group. The Host is furious, and it takes the Knight to get them to kiss and make up.

MAJOR CHARACTERS

The **Pardoner** is his own main character, since it is in the context of his personality that the tale takes on irony. He prides himself on being a practitioner of all the sins he preaches against, and plenty others besides. No wonder he's often seen as Chaucer's best psychological portrait. But unlike the Wife of Bath in her introduction, he is not presenting a justification for his life-style. He's saying how proud he is of his own deceptiveness.

Why would he disclose all his sordid tricks? Certainly they're not something to brag about, even when you're drunk, as he is. Some believe that years of hypocrisy have created an urge in him finally to admit his guilt; some think he wants to show off his love of money, or has stopped caring what others think; while others think he's simply totally unaware of how much he is revealing of his inner self.

He certainly embodies the theory of evil. Remember the picture of him from the General Prologue: a thin goat's voice, a suspiciously effeminate nature, and the assumption that a part of him is missing (he is either "gelding or mare," eunuch or homosexual). To the medieval mind, an absent part is a clear indication of moral deprivation; the inward and the outward are connected.

Is there any good at all in the Pardoner? Think about how Chaucer treats his characters, even the nasty ones, as human, as real people. For all his faults, the Pardoner at least is honest and knows he's damned to hell for his conniving. He is able to turn the villagers he dupes away from their greedy ways. And he tells us that when he stands in the pulpit and tells his lies, his hands and tongue go so fast that it's a "joy" to see his "business" *(line 71)*. You could see this as another example of his disgusting pride in himself, or as Chaucer's way of saying that even the lowest of the low can do something good. Also, there's a certain fascination in such an evil character. We wonder what makes him tick, and here he gives us an unusual opportunity to see behind the public mask he wears.

The **Three Rioters** have been seen as representing three major divisions of sin—perhaps gluttony, drunkenness, and blasphemy—three of the sins the Pardoner preaches against at the start of the tale. They aren't real characters, yet we get a clear picture of the way they carry on and live their lives. They are more stupid than evil.

The **Old Man** has been a mystery for centuries. Who is he? Death himself, the mythical Wandering Jew, merely an old man? Whoever he is, he serves the purpose of pointing the young men to the place where Death waits.

STORY LINE

Introduction

The Host asks the Pardoner for a joking story, but because of the kind of debauched man he is, the pilgrims are obviously afraid that he'll tell a bawdy story that's even worse than the Miller's. But before the Pardoner tells a moral tale, he must get drunk, "by St. Runyan." (This is a play on the Middle English word for "scrotum" ("runian"), in addition to being a saint's name.

The Pardoner boasts about being able to pull the wool over the eyes of the sheep, the villagers to whom he sells pardons. In bragging, does he reveal more of himself than he intends to? He tells about the "miracle" water that can cure jealousy, even in men who know their wives have slept with two or three priests *(line 43)*. In his tone of voice we can hear him laugh at those who, like him, are hypocrites in their religious calling. But does he mean to reveal his contempt for humanity as being as corrupt as he is? (For example, assuming that wives will cheat on their husbands, and with priests no less.) It's unclear.

He says three times that his sole purpose is to make money for himself. He has no desire to be like the Apostles and live in poverty or by hard work. Nonetheless, he can tell a moral tale with a smooth tongue, even without being moral himself. We get the impression he doesn't realize his own words, or care that he himself will go to hell for all the sins he warns others against. This is what gives his tale, like the Wife of Bath's, such poignancy: he is saying more about himself than he realizes.

The Tale

The young revelers are described enjoying "abominable" excesses—dancing girls, drinking, gambling, and tearing Christ to pieces in curses—and laughing at each other's sins. Just as we might be thinking that we're all a little like that sometimes, the Pardoner lights into a long attack against those very vices.

His longest is against drunkenness. He describes a drunken lout making loud snores that sound like "Sampson, Sampson" (line 226), and we remember that the Pardoner himself is effeminate and small-voiced in contrast. But the Pardoner is drunk, and this irony sheds doubtful light, not only on his tirade against drink, but also on the ones against gluttony, cursing, gambling, and lechery, since he's admitted to all of them.

All this makes us realize that while he doesn't care if the villagers' souls "go blackberrying" when they die, he doesn't care about his own spiritual condition either.

His tirades seem to have no particular logic to them, but he starts with the biggest, gluttony and drink, and proceeds downward. Each sin has moral examples attached; the cursing that accompanies the gambling section is especially vivid and funny—"By God's precious heart," "By his nails" (line 323).

He picks up the story of the three rioters as the main moral example.

NOTE: The point of view shifts here from the moralizing tone of the drunken Pardoner to Chaucer's own more objective point of view, since it concerns the selfishness and greed of men similar to the Pardoner.

The first sound we hear is a death bell as the corpse of one of their drinking buddies is carried past the door. But, like the Pardoner himself, the three are untouched by any morals that might be drawn.

The drunken three have an arrogant and prideful response—that they are capable of killing Death—but some also see something admirable in taking on such an adversary, even though it's just a drunken boast.

It's ironic that the three pledge their honor and vow to die for each other, calling each other "brother" and "friend," for they will soon be dying by each other's hand.

The old man they meet greets them meekly, but they respond impolitely, asking why he's still alive. His response, which includes a line from "Holy Writ" *(line 414)*, shows that he is patiently waiting for the will of God to die, since no youth will trade him his age. But the gamblers depend only on the momentary turns of fortune. The old man would trade all his belongings for a shroud *(line 406)*; by following his directions, the three revelers will do just that.

There's also a shift in the view of Death. From an evil being to be beaten or feared, the old man shows Death also as a welcome relief. Rather than being a "false traitor" as he is to the youths, Death is a natural part of life, and life itself may be "abominable" excess if lived too long.

He tells them Death awaits under a big oak tree, where they find the gold. Of course, because the theme of the sermon is that "money is the root of evil," we are meant to see that the money *is* Death, which symbolically is lying at the root of a tree. But the drunken rioters don't see that, even though ironically one of them says, "My wit is great, though I bourde [joke] and play" *(line 450).* He adds that they will spend the fortune as "lightly" as they've gotten it *(line 153).* Little does he know how true those words are.

But earthly goods create discord and greed, and God's ever-present plan, in the form of the Devil ("feend," *line 516),* appears in the conversation of the first two rioters and in the mind of the youngest. Unintentionally, in his guilt and nervousness, he tells the apothecary he needs the poison to kill "vermin," but we can see the irony; that's exactly what he and his false "friends" are.

As in the Knight's Tale, we're told that after the first two kill the youngest, one "happened," "per cas" (by chance) to drink the poisoned wine *(line 557).* This is our signal that it's anything but chance in the works. A divine plan is evident even in the evil schemes of these three fatal jokesters. They have found Death by carrying him around with them.

We're jolted by the change in tone when the Pardoner again intrudes his phony piety, telling people they are full of pride and blasphemy. Obviously he has memorized his tale and is just repeating it, not listening to a word he is saying about the wages of sin. Does all this mean that it doesn't matter how you act, you'll go to hell anyway? Or is there an assumption that even though the Pardoner is incorrigible, there's still hope for the rest of us? Either way, the Pardoner remains steadfast in his "cupiditas" (love of worldly things), and shows us the truth of his boast that he doesn't care about anything else when he offers fake pardons to his listeners.

We get this impression even when he ends by saying "I will not deceive you" *(line 590)* and that Christ's pardon is worth more than his. Does this mean the Pardoner is filled with a blast of true repentance? Readers have disagreed about this for years. You'll have to make up your mind based on what you have already seen of the character and his motives.

The Epilogue

Stepping down from his imaginary pulpit, the Pardoner becomes a mere man again, back to his old tricks of passing off "relics," which his traveling companions by now know better than to believe in. Even he knows it's ironic when he calls his presence on the trip a "suretee" (insurance, and also a legal bond) for the pilgrims.

But picking on the Host gets him more than he bargained for, reminding us forcefully that the tales are made up of remarkably lifelike and conflicting personalities. Perhaps he wants to get back at the Host for suggesting at the start that he tell a joking story instead of the sermons he prides himself on. For whatever reason, he tells the Host he should make the first offering for "he is most enveloped in sin." His next suggestion, "Unbuckle thy purse" *(line 617)*, has a sexual connotation that the Host, a burly bouncer of a guy, doesn't appreciate. The Host offers to use the Pardoner's testicles for relics, enshrined in a "hog's turd." Perhaps by calling attention to the Pardoner's physical and spiritual limitations, the Host's comments are meant to remind us of the gulf between the Pardoner's life and his tale.

It takes the Knight to restore harmony, which is fitting since he represents natural order and harmony. He makes the two kiss (another strange and hilarious sight, when you think about it) and the tale ends happily. But notice also that it's not the Pardoner, whose job it is to pardon, who forgives the Host for the crude remarks.

SOURCES

There's no one source for the Pardoner's Tale, but much of the philosophy comes again from Boethius, the early Christian philosopher. His view is that men are lifted up and thrown down by fickle fortune, but cannot see the divine plan beyond fortune's wheel. The plan, such as life or death, cannot be altered, so that even if the old man were to find someone to change places with him, he would not die until his time was due. The young men die because they are destined to die for their greed.

THEMES

1. VIEWS OF DEATH

We see Death first as the "thief" that the three revelers believe must be slain before he slays more people. This noble-sounding sentiment becomes ridiculous when you realize it's impossible to slay Death. The old man shows Death in another light, as an end to life that is part of the natural order and God's plan.

A third picture emerges at the deaths of the rioters, which is of righteous retribution. They went out looking for Death and they certainly found it. It's what they deserve for being fools and not following the right way of life.

The tale also deals with spiritual as well as actual death. The moral depth to which these young men descend is a kind of death that they can escape through correct living. But they don't, and so they meet physical death as well.

2. DIVINE ORDER

God's plan is evident in all things, even in the schemes of foolish drunks. It is obviously not an accident that they meet the old man who tells them where Death is, and that Death has been waiting for them. They think they can live life by their own rules; they can't see that the pattern is already destined.

3. DRUNKENNESS

A drunken man in medieval imagery represents one who keeps his eyes only on the lower, gross things of life instead of looking upward toward the grace of God. This image appears in other tales as well, such as the Knight's and Miller's, where men who lack foresight are compared to being "drunk as a mouse." Drunkenness, the Pardoner tells us in his sermon on the subject (while he is drunk), leads to other sins, such as lechery and gluttony.

4. PRIDE

Like the Pardoner himself, his characters exhibit pride, the kind that comes before a fall. To seek and try to kill Death is an attempt to go beyond the bounds of man, and therefore is punishable by death. What the Pardoner doesn't realize is that the moral of his tale is especially applicable to himself. He is as blind to that as his three revelers are.

FORM AND STRUCTURE

The introduction to the Pardoner's Tale is in the form of a sermon that he delivers complete with fancy flourishes to the poeple he tries to rook into buying pardons. His tale continues the format and launches into a series of "exempla," examples with a moral point that are richly illustrated and set down one after another. The story of the three rioters is an extended version of a moral example story, used often by preachers.

THE NUN'S PRIEST'S TALE

PLOT

In the introduction to the tale, the Knight interrupts the Monk and tells him to stop telling his tragic tales— they're annoying. The monk refuses to tell a different one, so the Host turns to the Nun's Priest, Sir John, and asks him to tell a merry tale. The priest obliges.

The story begins with a poor widow who supports herself and her two daughters as best she can by raising a few animals. She's contented because her desires are moderate; she wants no more than what she has.

The scene shifts to the yard, where Chanticleer the rooster, the best crower you've ever heard, rules over his seven hens. His favorite is Pertelote, who sings with him (this story takes place in the days when animals could speak and sing, we're told) and sits next to him on his perch at night.

Pertelote wakes before dawn to hear Chanticleer moaning in his sleep because of a nightmare. She asks what's wrong. He's afraid of the dream, in which a doglike animal wants to kill him. Pertelote taunts him for being afraid of a stupid dream, which doesn't mean anything. Bad dreams come from eating too much, she says, and offers to make him a laxative that will cure his nightmares.

Chanticleer launches into a long defense of dreams that foretell what will happen. But he ends by saying that with his fair lady by his side he is so filled with joy that he's not afraid of nightmares or dreams.

It's now daylight, so he ignores his fears and flies into the yard, mounting Pertelote twenty times by midmorning. But it's unfortunate that he took his wife's advice to dismiss his dream, for the fox is waiting for him in the bushes to carry him off.

The rooster is terrified, but the fox tells Chanticleer he doesn't mean to harm him. He has heard that he's a marvelous crower, as good as his father was. Chanticleer's father and mother, the fox says slyly, were once guests at his house. Could Chanticleer imitate his father's crowing?

Big headed from the flattery, Chanticleer closes his eyes to crow. As he stretches his neck, the fox grabs him, throws him across his back, and dashes off. The hens, cackling madly, begin the world's sorriest lament, which brings out the widow and her daughters. A chase scene ensues.

As they're running, Chanticleer tells the fox that if *he* were the fox, he'd turn and tell the crowd that it's too late, the bird is his. Good idea, says the fox, and of course as soon as he opens his mouth, Chanticleer escapes up into a tree. The fox tries to lure him down, but Chanticleer vows not to make the same mistake twice. The tale ends with the narrator warning that even though this is just a story about animals, there's a moral in it for people too.

In the epilogue the Host praises Sir John, not only for his tale, but for his manhood, making cracks about the hens he would need if he were a layman instead of a priest. The priest remains silent.

MAJOR CHARACTERS

We see the **widow** only briefly, at the beginning and near the end, but she represents an important aspect of the story. Her life is simple and contented because she feels none of the temptations we associate with rich living. We understand her life and moral values in just a few lines.

Chanticleer presents an immediate contrast to the widow's simplicity. He is described like the noble prince in courtly love romances, which is a ludicrous description of a rooster. But this portrait gives us insight into the lovable and not-so-lovable characteristics of us humans, who are just as proud and vain as he is.

As a rooster, he carries large responsibilities: he crows better than any other rooster, he thinks he's responsible for the very sunrise, he makes use of all the hens sexually, and he struts around his farmyard turf like a lion. He's proud to the point of being arrogant (remember that, especially in medieval literature, pride comes before a fall), he's aware of his attractiveness, he's intelligent and sly, he is full of joy and life.

Is it ridiculous to have all these noble and ignoble characteristics combined in a rooster? Does his chicken shape keep us from taking him seriously? You'll have to decide how much of his portrait is just for amusement and how much we should apply to ourselves.

Pertelote is a marvelous parody of a wife who henpecks her husband, in this case literally. Impressively, she can quote from Cato, a respected medieval authority, on dreams, which surely not many medieval wives could do, let alone chickens. But her interest lies mostly in the daily concerns of keeping her husband healthy and happy, chalking up his bad dream to indigestion, and offering a complicated mixture of herbs for a laxative.

She is more than this, though. She is presented as the beloved lady of medieval romances, the queenly figure for whom the knight would gladly die, in accordance with the ideal of courtly love. Yet Chanticleer teases her while serving her in a knightly fashion, implying that she doesn't know things that he knows and therefore shouldn't stick her beak in. But then he does listen to her, and ignores the warning of his dream and his own explanations.

You might examine whether she represents human folly, seeing only the base things in life and ignoring the spiritual realm, or if she stands for the practicality that Chanticleer lacks.

STORY LINE

We get a taste of the characters' symbolic importance to the tale. The widow's way of life, which takes the place of any physical description, is humbly Christian: she doesn't want what she can't have and she practices temperance in all things. This sets up the moral tone of the poem. But among her few possessions she does have a sheep named Moll. It's interesting that she and her daughters don't have names, but her sheep does. This prepares us for the introduction of animals that seem more human than the people in the tale.

Chanticleer appears more highly bred and privileged than the poor woman who owns him. He sees himself as the center of his small universe.

NOTE: Chaucer shifts the point of view here from the objective sight of the widow to the viewpoints of the barnyard. He gives a closeup description of Chanticleer and compares his comb to a "castle wall" *(line 40)*, making him appear large, as if we're seeing him on a hen's-eye level.

His portrait and that of the hens—his "paramours" *(line 47)*—are from a courtly romance, especially the standard romance description of Pertelote, "courteous, discreet, debonair," who captured the heart of this noble rooster when she was only seven days old. But the whole romantic ideal is undercut by a reminder that these are animals: we are in the long-ago days when animals and birds could speak and sing *(line 61)*. This shift back and forth from romance (and later, philosophy) to the barnyard occurs throughout the tale, usually with hilarious effect.

Chanticleer's dream is suggestive of a medieval riddle: what is like something and yet is not that thing? (You can probably think of similar riddles from childhood.) His nightmare is about an animal "like a dog," but he doesn't know what. We immediately recognize a fox, which obviously Chanticleer has never seen; this puts us in a position of knowing more than the rooster does and keeps us from taking him too seriously.

Pertelote then becomes anything but "courteous" and "debonair." It's ridiculous that he should be afraid of dreams, she says. Aren't you a man? she asks in all seriousness (though to us it's very funny). Dreams come from overeating, gas, and an imbalance of bodily humors, in her opinion, as does her husband's red "choler" (bile: one of the four temperaments believed to rule the body). In quoting Cato *(lines 120–121)*, she is presenting one prominent medieval view of dreams, the "natural" theory that says they are worthless. Her courtly tone of voice mixes with the pragmatic until she concludes he should take a laxative.

He thanks her courteously, then refutes her opinion. He uses "exempla"—highly structured examples that make a moral point—to show the theory that dreams are sent from heaven to point to joys and trials in the present life.

NOTE: Some readers think his courteous attitude here toward Pertelote is full of male superiority, barely masking his contempt for her intelligence. Keep this in mind; later we will see other attitudes toward women.

His first example, of two friends forced to sleep in different places, is long and serious. A man refuses to listen to the dream of his traveling companion saying he's being murdered, but it turns out to be true. The next is of another traveling pair, one of whom refuses to believe his friend's dream that they will be drowned, and he indeed gets drowned when the ship's bottom splits "accidentally."

In these examples, Chanticleer first brings up the idea of fortune, which "governs" us all equally *(lines 179–180)*. Is that the only purpose for his long-winded answer? It may be to build up suspense for the action to follow, or to create a serious purpose in contrast to the amusing fact that we're listening to a rooster. But it also serves to show that the point of the tale is basically serious. The change from comedy to a serious tone may represent the fact that fortune can change lives from cheerful to dismal, as indeed happens to Chanticleer later.

He rattles off half a dozen more short examples, in case Pertelote isn't convinced, or to impress everyone with his education. But after he predicts darkly that these ideas mean he will meet a terrible doom, he ends hilariously by adding that besides, he hates laxatives. This leads us to wonder whether his whole recitation has been from strongly held belief or from fear of having to take laxatives.

Returning to his courtly attitude, he tells Pertelote the sight of her takes away all his fears. Just as sure as "In principio" (the first words of the Bible; in other words, the gospel truth), "woman is man's joy and all his bliss" *(lines 343-346).*

NOTE: The pun is double and says something about Chanticleer's attitude toward his wife. The Latin quote really means, "Woman is man's confusion [or ruin]," and "In principio" ("In the beginning . . .") can also refer to the Fall in the beginning because of Eve. He could be mistranslating this to tease her or, as some believe, to hide his contempt for her. Or perhaps, being only a rooster, he doesn't understand it himself. Which do you think makes the most sense?

Chanticleer gives up his theories in favor of love, as the end of his speech indicates. But his decision to listen to Pertelote and ignore his own arguments about portentous dreams turns out to be a mistake.

Chanticleer's adventure takes place 32 days from the start of March (the beginning of the year, in those days), in other words, in May, the significance of which we saw in the Knight's Tale.

NOTE: The Nun's Priest's Tale interweaves many threads from other tales, leading many to believe that this is the story that most accurately shows Chaucer's own beliefs about humanity and its place in the grand scheme of things.

By calling attention to the start of the world "when God first made man" *(line 368)*, and remembering that the story takes place when animals could speak, Chaucer makes it sound like Chanticleer and his hens are close in time to the Fall and have a clearer vision than we have of where we all stand in God's grand design. We are again reminded of fortune: Chanticleer has a "sorrowful cas" (accident, a word Chaucer never uses lightly), and we are reminded of the biblical teaching that "worldly joy is soon gone" *(lines 384-386)*. This comes right after Chanticleer's announcement of contentment, warning us that only the higher pleasures of God are outside fortune's wheel. We're also reminded that the tone of the whole "romantic" tale is tongue-in-cheek when the narrator says the tale is just as "true" as the legend of Lancelot that women are so fond of. (Is this another slight against women?)

The fox's attack has been "forecast" *(line 397)* through Chanticleer's dream from God's "high imagination," and all the ideas presented so far now get put to the test of action. The narrator raises the whole idea of destiny and man's freedom as the catastrophe approaches, but in an exaggerated, humorous way. He brings up "simple" versus "conditional" necessity, an important argument with medieval scholars: does man live by "simple necessity," which means everything is predetermined, or by "conditional necessity," in which God knows everything but allows men freedom of choice?

Instead of answering, he puts the question in perspective by reminding us that this is a tale about a cock and a hen. Is this saying that philosophy is useless, and that the wisest of us know no more than barnyard animals? Some point to the confusion the narrator shows in the philosophical passage as evidence for this view. Others think it's just the Nun's Priest's way of avoiding responsibility for the philosophical explanation and for the attack on women that follows. (Is it Chaucer or the priest who decides to take back the offensive comments that women's advice is what caused the Fall?) The escape line *(line 442)* that he means these comments only as a joke might mean the narrator is part of the whole comedy of the tale, or that he's trying to make a fast getaway.

As the fox approaches, Chanticleer sings like a "mermaid" *(line 450)*, which in the Middle Ages symbolized the ancient Sirens whose sweet songs lured men to their doom. This is a reference to the fact that Chanticleer's voice will soon do him in. He's about to learn the difference between believing something (that his dream spelled evil to come) and acting on that belief, which he hasn't done. Because this is a tale with a Christian moral, he must deal with the trials and tribulations arising from his action (or lack of it) before he can reach a happy ending.

When he sees the fox, he feels an instinct to flee, because it is in the natural order for an animal to run from its enemy. This instinctive knowledge flies in the face of all the learned knowledge we've been shown, and shows the divine order as it really is—all things according to their nature.

Chanticleer falls prey not only to the fox but to the sin of pride, emphasized by the fox's use of Devil (saying he's not a "fiend," *line 466*) and angel (saying that Chanticleer sings as merrily as one, *line 472*), which refers to Satan's fall from grace. On another level, it's possible that the fox's use of flattery and deceit to win Chanticleer parallels the rooster's use of the same tactics to woo his wife. His crowing (which also means "boasting") also becomes ironic when we realize that the fox is praising Chanticleer's "wisdom and discretion" *(line 498)*, which the bird certainly is not displaying at this moment. He's literally blinded by flattery because he's closed his eyes to sing.

The exclamation of complaint that follows is hilarious, attaching such heroic importance to the abduction of a rooster: "Alas, that Chanticleer flew from the beams!" Venus is implored to save her noble servant (like Palamon in the Knight's Tale and like the Wife of Bath who also loves "more for delight than to multiply the world," *line 524*). The passage might also serve to ridicule the learned works and show how useless they are when it comes to keeping men (or roosters) from the consequences of their own stupidity.

The chase scene that follows starts with a joke of the hens' laments being worse than when the Romans burned Carthage and Nero burned Rome. This could serve to point up Chanticleer's inflated sense of his own importance, or just to make the hens again appear more human. The scene also brings the spectator right into the mess—out "ran Colle our dog" *(line 563)*.

There's no longer any control or reasoned argument, just chaos. There's even a reference to a wider uproar, the Peasants Revolt headed by Jack Straw *(line*

574), when many people feared for their lives because of rioting in the streets. Like the animals in the poem, there was good reason to fear that heaven would fall.

Suddenly the priest tells us, "See how Fortune suddenly turns around the hope and pride of their enemy!" (lines 583-584). Chanticleer has flattered his wife, then the fox wins him by flattery, now he uses flattery to win his freedom back; a nicely completed circle of fortune. The whole idea of running off at the mouth—referring to Chanticleer's use of the dream "knowledge" that is true but that he ignores—also gets pegged when the fox says misfortune will come to those who blab when they should shut up (lines 613-615).

Chanticleer sees the truth through this self-awareness, learning from his mistakes. The sins of pride and self-satisfaction are solved by self-knowledge. And, in case we're tempted just to write off the whole tale as a "folly" (trifle) about a fox, a rooster, and a hen, the Nun's Priest reminds us we should "Take the moral, good people." We should accept what applies to us (take the "fruit" and leave the "chaff," line 623) and become better people for it.

SETTING

The widow's little cottage provides us the moral as well as the physical setting for the tale. Her way of life provides a hint of ideal human, Christian behavior that leads to self-restraint and contentment. This is the world to which Chanticleer's boastful self-importance is connected, and the world to which the barnyard returns after the intrusion of the evil fox.

STYLE

As in the Miller's Tale, we get an ironic use of the language of courtly love and description to point up human desires and weaknesses, which the ideal of courtly love embodies. (Weakness because the beloved lady has the power of life or death over the lovesick knight, as in the Knight's Tale.)

The "noble" style also serves to parody the tragic tone of the Monk's endless tales of Fortune bringing down all the greats (Hercules, Samson, etc.), and supplies a comic answer to his gloom. (Keep in mind, too, that the Knight requests another tale, so perhaps the Nun's Priest means to give the Knight something to match his noble taste.) The parody of a classical tragic style also gives us reasons for the occasional outbursts of lament and complaint (such as the wonderful "death" passage that begins, "O woeful hens!" *line 549*).

Themes of other tales, such as the ones just mentioned, appear through the tone and language of this tale. Some take this to mean that the Nun's Priest, who is never described, and "Chaucer" the narrator, who also is left blank, are pretty much the same person. This may or may not be true, but we can see a great deal of affection for the attitudes expressed here, especially since Chaucer has a soft spot for Boethius, whose philosophy plays a role in several of these tales.

Another reason for the humorous tone of the story could be that Chaucer accepts his world with an unshakable faith in divine order that underlies the world's craziness. Humor allows him to be detached from ups and downs of the characters (and making them birds is another way of detaching himself). Because he is so sure of God's providence, he can calmly watch other people's shortcomings and even his own.

THEMES

1. DREAMS

The relevance and importance of dreams, like the relevance of astrology and dreams/visions in the Miller's Tale, still provoke lively debate today. Is Chanticleer's dream valid in the Freudian sense—dealing with anxiety and wish-fulfillment—or is it, as some would still believe, a psychic way of revealing the future? Chauticleer gives us plenty of ammunition for believing that dreams can tell the future, but do you believe his stories? Does the fact that his dream does come true give more weight to the psychic idea? Or is the dream another way of showing that everything in the world is predetermined and man's actions are pointless?

2. DESTINY AND FREE WILL

This is a complex issue that is brought up in the tale but not resolved. We are told two contradictory things: that man is free to make his own choices (as Chanticleer is free to accept or reject Pertelote's advice), and that he is not free because everything is already destined (which means the fox will attack no matter whose advice Chanticleer follows). Both ideas are right, but neither is completely right. That's the problem of being human.

3. HUMAN RESPONSIBILITY

This ties in with destiny, as all the themes interweave in this tale. Man is responsible to a divine plan and, on a romantic level, responsible to love and honor. Chanticleer feels he must answer to his wives as well as take care of his own business of crowing and sovereignty over the barnyard.

4. LEARNING FROM EXPERIENCE

This is what separates humans from animals since, in this sense, Chanticleer and Pertelote and the fox are as human as they come. The wisdom that the rooster and fox learn from experience goes beyond the natural order of things into the higher realm of God's good, where they, like we, learn a "moral." As the end of the tale states, all that is written is written for our "doctrine" (learning, and also church doctrine).

5. KINDS OF LOVE

The language of courtly love emphasizes the sensual animal love that Chanticleer has for Pertelote. According to courtly tradition, this is the love through which a knight perfects himself and wins grace from his lady. But at the same time we get scattered references to woman as man's destruction and responsible for Adam's fall. Even where the narrator thinks better of his attack on women (after all, he's speaking in front of his "boss," the Prioress, the other nuns, and the imposing Wife of Bath), the words are there for us to consider. The kinds of love can't be resolved, but they're both there.

6. DECEPTION AND PRIDE

Chanticleer allows himself to be deceived by the fox because he is flattered and proud of his singing ability, which he believes even makes the sun rise *(line 38)*. He also deceives Pertelote, in mistranslating the Latin saying about women, to impress her and boost his estimation in her eyes (at least, this has been argued). Because of pride he falls and learns his lessons the hard way.

7. ATTITUDES TOWARD WOMEN

Are women the cause of the Fall, as Chanticleer and the narrator hint, however jokingly, or are they indeed "man's bliss"? We are given indications of both attitudes, since Chanticleer does "fall" by following the urgings of his practical wife, but he also attributes all the joy in his life to her love. He is called a servant of Venus, because he follows love with such devotion, but he also follows God, believing that his dream is sent from heaven. Each belief would indicate a different attitude toward women.

THE OTHER TALES

THE REEVE'S TALE

Oswald the Reeve, who is a carpenter, takes offense at the Miller's tale about a cuckolded carpenter, and says he'll pay him back in "force"—in the same coarse language and even in the same form (the French bawdy fabliau). The Reeve also gripes because the Miller's carpenter, like the Reeve, is an old man who can only talk about the things he can't do anymore. (Like his enemy, the Reeve is concerned with sexual matters.)

The rowdy tale concerns a miller who steals grain, especially from a Cambridge college that takes its corn to him to be ground. Once, when the miller has stolen more than usual because no one's there to watch him, two students, Alan and John, decide to oversee the grinding. The miller decides he can outwit the students despite their highclass education. He unties their horse, and while Alan and John chase after it, the miller steals half their grain. By the time the horse is caught, it's dark and the students are forced to ask the miller to put them up. He does, although there's only one room. The miller and his wife are in one bed, the students are in another, and the miller's twenty-year-old daughter is in a third. To get even with the miller for playing a trick on them, one of the students sleeps with the daughter, and the other with the wife, who thinks she is sleeping with the miller! When the miller finds out, he starts beating up Alan. The wife, thinking the two students are fighting, slams the miller on the head with a stick. The beating and cuckolding, says the Reeve, is what the miller deserves for being such a liar and cheat.

As in the Miller's Tale, justice is done to those who deserve it, more or less. While the actions in the Reeve's Tale are just as farfetched as in the Miller's Tale, it is not as rollicking and funny, just as the Reeve is not as loud and boisterous as the Miller.

THE COOK'S TALE

Roger, the Cook, enjoys the Reeve's Tale so much he promises to top it with an even dirtier one that he swears is true. The Host warns kiddingly it had better be good to repay the pilgrims for the reheated pies the Cook has sold them. (As you see, payment is an important theme in this opening series of tales, which ends with this one.)

The Cook's Tale can barely be called one, since it only consists of the opening lines. (Maybe Chaucer decided two dirty stories in a row was enough.) The Cook starts to tell of an apprentice cook, Perkin Reveler (Partyer) who'd rather dance, drink, and fool around than tend shop. His boss, worrying that this rotten apple could spoil the whole barrel (it was an old saying even then!), fires Perkin, who moves in with a friend who has the same wild habits. This friend has a wife who runs a shop as a front for her sexual goings-on. This is where the tales ends. (You might wish for it to continue!)

THE MAN OF LAW'S TALE

Seeing that the day is almost a quarter over, the Host urges the Man of Law to tell a story, but the lawyer claims Chaucer already has covered all the best subjects in his poems (is Chaucer self-advertising here?). Nonetheless, the Man of Law prefaces his tale with a tirade against poverty, praising rich merchants who make and hoard their money.

The tale, taken from an earlier fourteenth-century historian named Nicholas Trivet, is about Constance, the almost unbelievably long-suffering daughter of the Roman Emperor. She becomes engaged to the Sultan of Syria, a Muslim who vows to convert himself and his subjects to Christianity in order to marry Constance. It is an arranged marriage (the custom among royal families almost to this day), and Constance accepts it with great patience. The Sultan's mother, angry at her son's rejection of Islam, plans to have all the Christians murdered, including the Sultan, at the wedding feast. Constance is sent adrift on the sea.

She lands in Northumberland in England, and she is taken in by a constable and his wife, both pagans. Constance converts them to Christianity but a knight sent by Satan kills the wife and plants the murder on Constance. He is mysteriously struck dead when he testifies against her, and the pagan king, Alla, is converted by the miracle and marries Constance. Again an evil royal mother intervenes to have their child killed, so Constance and her son return to the sea. They end up in Rome, eventually reunited with King Alla. Constance is also reunited with her father the Emperor.

The tale is punctuated with commentary by the
Man of Law, which helps us see the tale is partly
intended as an allegory. Constance personifies the
virtues of patience, loyalty ("constance") and accep-
tance of God's will despite incredible suffering. The
allegory form, extremely popular in Chaucer's day,
exaggerates Constance's virtues and her misfortunes
to make a moral point about aspiring toward Christian
perfection.

THE FRIAR'S TALE

The Friar offers a tale about a summoner, his professional enemy since summoners were members of
the secular clergy and he, a friar, was a member of the
regular clergy, outside the secular clergy's jurisdic-
tion. The Host asks the Friar not to insult the Summoner but the Summoner promises to repay him.

The tale is a medieval version of spies, double
agents and blackmail, just as popular with Chaucer's
audience as thrillers are with us today. A corrupt
young summoner, whose job is to bring people into
church court for religious offenses, has a network of
stoolpigeons and prostitutes to spy on people and
lure them into sin. He then extorts bribes from his
victims to keep their slates clean. On his way to take
money from an old woman, he meets a man as sleazy
as himself, with whom he joins in partnership. The
stranger—who has exactly the same characteristics as
the summoner and even looks like him—admits he's
a devil. The summoner, suddenly and ironically honorable, sticks to their pact. We learn that the devil
can't damn anyone unless the curse is truly meant, so
when the old woman cries, "the Devil take you," the
fiend asks if she means it. She does, unless the sum-

moner repents, which he won't, so he is instantly whisked off to hell. The point, says the Friar, is that summoners should become honest men.

The tale is similar to the Pardoner's Tale in being a lesson of sorts. The character of the sex-and-tavern loving Friar, whom Chaucer pretends to admire in the Prologue, is matched by the hypocritical character in his story, who, like the Friar, can't see that certain low-life characteristics apply to him. The joke is as much on the Friar as it is on the Summoner.

THE SUMMONER'S TALE

The Summoner is so furious he shakes like a leaf, and retaliates first by mentioning a friar whose vision of hell includes seeing millions of friars swarming around the Devil's rear end.

The tale, grosser than the tale he's trying to pay back, is of a friar who is hypocrisy personified. Visiting a rich but sick man named Thomas, the friar gives a long sermon against anger, getting angrier as he goes on; against gluttony, having just asked Thomas's wife for an enormous meal; and in praise of poverty, while urging Thomas to give the friars all his money. He also pretends to have offered prayers he never delivered. Thomas, furious at being duped, tells the friar to reach for something hidden down his (Thomas') pants, then farts on him. The friar, like a spoiled child, runs to the lord and tells on Thomas, but the general consensus is that Thomas should share his "wealth" with the other friars as well!

This pay-back scheme compares to the Miller and Reeve in one-upsmanship vulgarity. But the humor here also lies in the Summoner's use of scholarly religious discourse as a gross subject.

THE CLERK'S TALE

The Host tells the thoughtful Clerk to cheer up and tell a lively story. The Clerk agrees, saying his tale comes from the Italian poet Petrarch (who lived at the same time as Chaucer).

Griselda is a beautiful, virtuous peasant woman whom the king, Walter, decides to marry. She is obedient to his every wish, but Walter develops an overriding need to test her patience and loyalty. First he takes their first child, a baby girl, and later their son. He lets Griselda believe the children have been killed, though in fact he has sent them to another town. Finally he says she's too low-class, so he sends her back to her poor father—then brings her back to the palace to help in preparations for his marriage to a new, nobly-born wife! In fact, he has sent for the children's return, and Griselda doesn't know the new "bride" is really her daughter. Walter reveals the children's identities, and restores Griselda to the throne, convinced at last of her patience and fortitude. Through the whole thing Griselda doesn't complain once.

This tale, like the Man of Law's, is a long ode (based on Petrarch's distillation of a Boccaccio story) to a single virtue, in this case patience. Like Constance, Griselda is almost saintlike in her embodiment of virtue. But though you might be tempted to dismiss Griselda as a doormat, notice that this tale is an answer to the Wife of Bath's argument that women should control a marriage. Griselda and Walter both exhibit single-mindedness, Walter in his determination to test his wife, Griselda in her steadfast patience. Perhaps they're better suited to each other than we thought at first!

THE MERCHANT'S TALE

The Merchant admits his wife is hardly like Grisel-da; in fact, his two months of marriage have been hell. His tale, therefore, ties in with his character because it tells of the pitfalls of expecting too much of a marriage.

January, a rich knight, turns sixty and suddenly decides to marry. He lists examples of "good" women, all of whom ironically were responsible for a man's downfall. He gets pro and con advice from two friends, Justinus ("just one") and Placebo ("flatterer"), the "just" man arguing against and the other for. January settles on young May (the winter/spring distinction) as his bride, and enjoys his wedding night although Chaucer makes him look rather foolish. May falls for Damian, a young squire who is sick with love for her; January suddenly goes blind and won't let May leave his side. In January's walled garden, May arranges for Damian to climb a certain pear tree. Telling January she's climbing the tree to get him a pear, she scampers up. Meanwhile, the gods—Pluto and his wife Proserpina—take male and female sides in the argument. Pluto has January's sight return just as May and Damian embrace in the tree; Proserpina provides May with a fast-talking excuse, that January's eyes are deceiving him since he is still unused to the light.

The tale echoes the Miller's in the plot of old man/ young wife and her plans for infidelity. Chaucer combines standard medieval set-ups (the age difference; the view of arguing gods, as in the Knight's Tale; the walled garden; and the pear tree, symbolizing sex) for a tale that is almost allegorical but carries a bitter tone because of the Merchant's own situation.

THE SQUIRE'S TALE

The Squire refuses to tell a love story but says he'll tell something as best he can.

The tale, unfinished, is a mystical one about a magical horse, mirror, ring, and sword that Gawain, an unknown knight, presents to the king of Tartary at a feast. The brass horse can fly anywhere; the mirror can show past, future, or any lover's unfaithfulness; the ring gives the wearer knowledge of the birds' language; the sword cuts through anything. The ring is given to Canacee, the king's daughter, who wears it into the garden and uses it to hear a sad female hawk who has been jilted by her lover. Canacee nurses the hawk back to health. The Squire then promises to tell of the other magic gifts, of battles and the king and his sons, but the Franklin interrupts.

The Squire's personality is reflected in this rambling tale because he has travelled to the Far East, where the tale takes place, and is a devoted follower of courtly love. Like his father the Knight, he packs his tale with description and detail of wonderful occult events from Eastern folk tales, with a smattering of Arthurian legend.

THE FRANKLIN'S TALE

The Franklin compliments the Squire's qualities and wishes his son were more like him. His tale, though, won't be as colorful or as well-spoken as the Squire's, since he is a plain speaker.

He tells of the faithful Dorigen who is grief-stricken when her husband, Arveragus, goes away to battle. While he's gone, she paces the rockstrewn Brittany cliffs. She doesn't know that Aurelius, a squire living nearby, is madly in love with her, which he finally tells her. She rejects him, but he's so upset that she kiddingly says she'll love him when he makes all the rocks on the coast disappear. Knowing that's impossible, Aurelius falls ill from unrequited love and stays in bed for two years, while Arveragus returns to his happy wife. But Aurelius' brother, worried, knows a magician to whom Aurelius promises 1000 pounds if he can make the rocks disappear. The magician creates the illusion that they're gone, and Dorigen is horrified when she learns she must keep her promise. She tells her husband what has happened. Faithful to his knightly sense of honor, Arveragus insists she keep her promise. But when Dorigen sadly goes to Aurelius, he is so impressed with Arveragus' nobility that he sends her home. Meanwhile, Aurelius can't afford to pay the rest of the money he owes the magician. The magician, in turn, is moved by the story and tells Aurelius to forget the money. The Franklin ends by asking, Which of these is the most noble gentleman?

The tale is rich in symbols and wordplay. Dorigen's marriage is based on "trouthe" (truth, loyalty), the first virtue of the Knight whom Chaucer idealizes in the Prologue. Marriage here is a sensible middle ground between the Wife of Bath's idea of domination and the Clerk's notion of total submission. The loosely-adapted *breton lai* (Brittany tale) is based on Boccaccio and brings up questions of promises and inner nobility.

THE PHYSICIAN'S TALE

Virginius, a rich, noble knight, has a beautiful daughter, Virginia, whom Nature has blessed with a nearly perfect body. She is the picture of virtue (the Physician here inserts a lecture about bringing up children). An evil judge, Appius, sees Virginia and wants to have her, but knows he must resort to underhandedness to get her. He gets a local scoundrel, Claudius, to say in court that Virginia was actually his servant girl whom Virginius had stolen from his house years before. Before Virginius can protest, Appius announces he will take Virginia as a ward of the court. Rather than submit, Virginius tells his dauther she must die, which she accepts. When Virginius brings his daughter's head to Appius, the judge orders that he be hanged. But a crowd, furious at the judge's treachery, throws him into jail where he hangs himself. Claudius' life is spared only because Virginius pleads for him; instead, he's exiled.

The tale, about "the wages of sin," comes from Livy, the Roman historian. But Chaucer gets it through the French *Romance of the Rose*, which he translated. The tale is somewhat appropriate to the Physician, who spends a great deal of time describing the way Nature has created Virginia's perfect anatomy, perhaps out of professional interest. (The passage takes the form of a classical statement by the Goddess Nature, who helps God in creation.)

THE SHIPMAN'S TALE

A rich merchant with a beautiful wife loves entertaining guests, one of whom is a young monk who grew up in the same village as the merchant. During a visit, the monk comes across the wife in the garden while the husband is in the countinghouse. Swearing him to secrecy, the wife tells how miserable she is, lacking the things women want in their husbands (health, wisdom, riches, generosity, affection, and sex). She then asks the monk to lend her 100 francs that she can't get from her stingy husband. He agrees on the condition that she promise to sleep with him while the husband's away. Before the merchant leaves, the monk asks for a 100-franc loan, which the merchant gladly gives. The monk passes the money to the wife, who goes to bed with him. Later, the merchant visits the monk, who says he's repaid the money to the wife. Returning home, the merchant scolds the wife for not telling him about the returned loan; the wife replies she didn't know it was a loan and spent the money on clothes. The merchant decides he has no choice but to forgive the wife.

The tale, a fabliau like the Miller's and Reeve's tales, may have originally been intended for a female pilgrim. There's certainly a connection between the wife's words on husbands and the Wife of Bath's question about what women want. But the crass language and heavy dose of sexual punning fits the character of the shady Shipman; so does the assumption that it's okay for the monk to violate his vow of celibacy and take advantage of the merchant's friendship.

THE PRIORESS' TALE

The Prioress opens with a hymn to the Virgin Mary, praising her virtues, to introduce a tale in which Mary plays a part.

The tale takes place in a large city with a Jewish quarter. A little boy who loves the Virgin Mary has to walk through the Jewish ghetto to school, where he learns to sing *Alma redemptoris*, a Latin hymn praising Mary. The Jews conspire to have him killed, and his body, with throat cut, is found in an outhouse the next day by his frantic mother. A miracle occurs: the boy, slit throat and all, starts to sing the hymn he's memorized. When questioned by the abbot, the dead boy says the Virgin Mary put a grain on his tongue, and he won't die until it is removed. The abbot takes it off and the child gives up the ghost. The Jews are dragged by horses, then killed. The Prioress ends with a reference to St. Hugh of Lincoln, allegedly murdered by Jews a century earlier.

It's argued that the Prioress' gentle description in the Prologue is sarcastic in light of this anti-Semitic tale; others say Chaucer is merely repeating an attitude toward Jews that was common in the medieval Church. Perhaps he intends irony in the fact that the Prioress laments over the boy and not the Jews, and that her violent tale is written in the form of a popular pious story praising the Virgin Mary (appropriate for a nun like the Prioress, who sees herself, like many nuns, under Mary's protection).

TALE OF SIR TOPAS

The Host asks Chaucer, the narrator, for a tale, describing him in the process as chubby, short (like an elf) and always looking down. (We don't know if this is how Chaucer really looked!) Chaucer promises the only tale he says he knows in rhyme.

Sir Topas is a good-looking knight, talented, whom ladies sigh for (but he stays chaste). One night he dreams of an elf queen and vows to ride to the ends of the earth to find her. He meets a giant whom he promises to fight the next day. . . . Here the tale is interrupted by the Host, who can't stand these horrible rhymes any more. So instead, Chaucer offers a "little" story in prose, which threatens to be as boring as Sir Topas!

The irony is that Chaucer would assign himself such a weak tale, filled with "knight-meets-fair-maiden" clichés that were old even then. It's written in a popular, bouncy rhythm, but even those of us unfamiliar with the style can see the tale is a spoof on romances. Even the stock description of Sir Topas (topaz symbolized chastity, by the way) is a joke.

THE TALE OF MELIBEUS

Chaucer wades through a sermon about whether it's better to avenge violence with more violence, or agree to peaceful settlement. The argument is between Sir Melibeus (pro-violence) and his wife Dame Prudence (anti-violence) who are deciding what action to take against three thieves who brutally wound their daughter. Peaceful methods prevail, but the "tale" is more moralistic wrangling than plot.

The tale is translated almost word for word from a French tale that in turn comes from Latin. The point is the philosophical arguments, not the narrative, so it's generally regarded as a clunker. This is ironic, because it is Chaucer who tells it.

THE MONK'S TALE

After receiving some grief from the Host about his probable "hunting" of women (see Prologue), the Monk agrees to tell a tale—but it's not lively, as the Host hoped.

The Monk details the tragedies of sixteen famous men and one woman, their lives and downfalls: seven connected with the Old Testament (Lucifer, Adam, Samson, Nebuchadnezzar, Balthasar, Holofernes, Antiochus); five from the classics (Hercules, Nero, Julius Caesar, Alexander, Croesus); and five from history (Queen Zenobia, Kings Peter of Spain and of Cyrus, Bernardo of Lombardy, Ugolino of Pisa). He says he has one hundred tragedies to relate, but the Knight interrupts him.

The tragedy form was popular in the Middle Ages; this one comes from Boccaccio. Like Chaucer's tales, these are fairly monotonous tragedies and the moral—that Fortune takes away as well as gives—is obvious.

THE SECOND NUN'S TALE

To combat idleness, which encourages vice and the devil, the Second Nun offers a translation of the life of St. Cecilia. She invokes a prayer to the Virgin Mary to help her present the tale.

Cecilia of Rome wishes to remain a virgin but is promised in marriage to Valerian, a pagan. On their wedding night she tells him anyone who touches her will be killed by her guardian angel. He wants proof (wouldn't you!), but she says he must first go to Pope Urban and be baptized. He goes and a vision appears. Convinced, he returns to find an angel with roses and lilies with Cecilia. Eventually Valerian's brother is also baptized, and both are caught and die martyrs' deaths. Cecilia too is supposed to die but she lives for three days after the pagans try to cut off her head. Pope Urban buries and canonizes her, and turns her house into a church.

The tale is in the popular form of a legend about a saint's life, as you might expect from a nun. This version of St. Cecilia's life is from Latin, and includes devices often found in legends, such as derivations of the meaning of the saint's name, which in this case are mostly wrong.

THE CANON'S YEOMAN'S TALE

Two strangers ride up, one in black, assumed to be a Canon (a churchman connected with a cathedral) and his Yeoman (servant), who has an odd-colored face, he says, from blowing in the fire. It turns out that the Canon is an alchemist (who tries to turn other metals into gold, usually in fire, a process which early medieval society believed happened naturally over time). The Canon dashes away in shame, but the Yeoman rambles on about the technical jargon the alchemists use, about how none of the experiments work, and about how, at this rate, he'll never get out of debt.

The tale is about a crooked alchemist who fools a priest into thinking he really can turn baser (lower) metals into gold. Through a series of tricks, he makes gold and silver appear out of coals and wax in the fire, and the priest is so impressed he buys the alchemist's "secret" formula for forty pounds. Needless to say, the alchemist does one more "magic" trick—he disappears, fast. The Yeoman then knocks the field of alchemy and ends with a mess of technical nonsense.

The tale is hard going for anyone who isn't an expert in alchemist terminology. Even by Chaucer's day, alchemy was considered by most to be a fake science, and many clerics disapproved of it as contrary to God's will.

THE MANCIPLE'S TALE

The Host asks the Manciple for his tale while the pilgrims are busy trying to keep the drunken Cook on his horse.

A man named Phoebus embodies every virtue—gentleness, kindness, bravery—but is very jealous of the wife he loves dearly. He has a white-feathered crow that can speak, and when he goes away, the wife's lover comes over. When Phoebus returns, the crow tells all. In a jealous rage, Phoebus kills his wife, then regrets it bitterly. Angry now at the bird for opening its beak, Phoebus pulls its white feathers and changes them for black, takes away the bird's voice, and kicks it out. The tale ends with advice against wicked gossip, in favor of keeping your tongue.

The tale is retold from a well-known fable in Ovid's *Metamorphoses*. (As in classical times, tales revolving around why something is so—here, the crow's black feathers and raucous voice—were popular in the Middle Ages.) It's the shortest of all the complete tales, perhaps because Chaucer meant the Manciple to take his own advice about keeping his words down to a minimum!

THE PARSON'S TALE

The Host urges the Parson to be quick, since it's dusk, but the Parson produces a long sermon in prose about the Seven Deadly Sins, not really a tale at all.

The Parson touches on penitence, confession, grace, pride, envy, anger, laziness, greed, gluttony and lechery. His lengthy sermon, which most people probably wouldn't sit through in church, nevertheless ties together all the arguments of the other pilgrims by putting them on a higher plane, and serves as a fitting end to the Tales. His tale emphasizes the spiritual values underlying the pilgrimage.

Like the Knight, the Parson is an ideal figure, so it also makes sense that one should begin the Tales and the other end them. However, because of the plodding and unpoetic quality of the Parson's Tale, some readers doubt it is written by Chaucer. Take a look and see for yourself how it compares with the other tales.

CHAUCER'S RETRACTION

At the end Chaucer puts in a modest note asking readers to forgive him if there's anything in the tales they disapprove of. Anything displeasing, Chaucer says, comes from my lack of ability, since I'd have said it better if I could. (Yet at the start he tells us he has no choice but to write exactly what the pilgrims say!) He asks God to pray for him and forgive him the "worldly vanities" he has written or translated: *Troilus and Criseyde*, the *House of Fame*, *Parliament of Fowls*, *Book of the Duchess*, and other "lecherous" tales, even the *Canterbury Tales*. He revokes them all, asking Christ and Mary to save him on Judgment Day. It's not clear why Chaucer wrote this, but it serves again to remind us of the ultimate seriousness of Chaucer's tales and faith.

A STEP BEYOND

Tests and Answers

TESTS

Test 1

1. The Knight   _____
   A. sang bawdy songs
   B. was one of the most respected of the pilgrims
   C. was an excellent woodsman, dressed in green

2. The Prioress' gold brooch bore the   _____ inscription
   A. *Honi soit qui mal y pense*
   B. *Nil sine magno laborum*
   C. *Amor vincit omnia*

3. The Monk spent a good deal of time   _____
   A. in fasting and doing penance
   B. justifying his extra-ecclesiastical activities
   C. extracting money from his congregants

4. The various guildsmen were represented by   _____ the
   A. Haberdasher, the Dyer, and the Weaver
   B. Shipman, the Carpet Maker, and the Franklin
   C. Reeve, the Carpenter, and the Manciple

5. In describing the Doctor of Physic, Chaucer   _____ mentioned his special
   A. affection for gold
   B. affinity for the Bible
   C. ability to cure illness

6. The pilgrim who frequently quoted authorities   _____
on love was the
A. Friar   B. Summoner
C. Wife of Bath

7. In the General Prologue, Chaucer relied   _____
heavily on
A. scholarship and wit
B. subtlety and irony
C. sophistication and mood creation

8. The pilgrim with the fiery red complexion and   _____
the garlic breath was the
A. Reeve   B. Summoner   C. Pardoner

9. One could buy indulgences from the   _____
effeminate
A. Pardoner   B. Manciple   C. Franklin

10. According to Chaucer's original plan, the   _____
pilgrims would have told
A. 58 tales   B. 87 tales   C. 120 tales

11. In the Knight's Tale, Arcite and Palamon pin their
hopes for winning love on fortune. Explain.

12. Why is Theseus often seen as the main character of the
Knight's Tale? Use examples.

13. How is the Miller's tale of bawdiness a moral story?

Test 2

1. Many of the pilgrims had   _____
A. mental problems
B. psychosomatic complaints
C. physical ailments

2. The Knight's Tale dealt with   _____
A. an old carpenter from Oxford
B. chivalry and ideal love
C. immorality and poetic justice

3. The perfect woman, Constance, was _____
   celebrated in the
   A. Cook's Tale
   B. Man of Law's Tale
   C. Clerk's Tale

4. The Introduction that is longer than the actual _____
   tale is the
   A. Wife of Bath's prologue
   B. Prioress' prologue
   C. Miller's prologue

5. The outspoken traveler with interesting _____
   opinions about marriage and celibacy was
   the
   A. Wife of Bath   B. Nun's Priest
   C. Merchant

6. The Reeve and the Summoner told their tales _____
   in order to
   A. introduce a note of `levity between two
      serious stories
   B. impress the travelers with their personal
      bravery
   C. repay someone else

7. Balance for the Wife of Bath's woman was _____
   provided by
   A. the maiden Dorigen
   B. Patient Griselda
   C. Innocent Rebecca

8. Chaucer's language is characterized by _____
   A. double entendres
   B. clever puns
   C. sparkling metaphors

9. Chanticleer, the talking rooster, was _____
   victimized by
   A. his lady, Pertelote

B. the Nun's Priest

C. the sly fox

10. The Canterbury Tales end unusually with _____ Chaucer's

   A. comic epilogue

   B. retraction

   C. farewell to Harry Bailey, the Host

11. In the Pardoner's Tale, what is the connection between the three revelers and the old man?

12. Explain how the Pardoner's prologue gives the tale its irony.

13. Why is the hero of the Nun's Priest's Tale a chicken?

ANSWERS

Test 1

1. B   **2.** C   **3.** B   **4.** A   **5.** A   **6.** C

7. B   **8.** B   **9.** A   **10.** C

11.   The two knights can change their imprisoned state, but only if fortune smiles on them. Remember when Arcite is sighing that Palamon has all the luck because he is in jail, while Palamon moans that Arcite is so fortunate because he is free? Both depend on outer forces to free them: Arcite on Perotheus' love and Theseus' mercy, Palamon on "a friend" *(line 610)* to break out of prison. Fortune is the roller coaster that men see as the agent that satisfies or denies their desires.

But we're told that things happen because of fate *(line 608).* That is the truth behind fortune, which men can't see but only guess. That's why, when Palamon asks Venus for Emelye's love while Arcite petitions Mars, each thinks he has received a sign that he will win. In fact, the end is already determined, as we see in the scene between Saturn and the other gods/planets.

12. Theseus represents the order and justice of the divine order, a justice that is tempered with mercy. Examples of his mercy includes letting the two Theban knights live, letting Arcite go free, and letting them live a second time. We see his compassion as far more objective than the selfish, almost childish squabbling that goes on between the two knights. Another indicator is that Theseus sets great store by ritual and ceremony, which are symbols of order in the world.

13. The Miller's Tale, for all its crudeness, sticks to the idea that there is a right and wrong way to do things. Alison may be wrong in choosing Nicholas over Absalom, or in choosing anyone at all other than her husband, but each of them gets his just deserts based on his actions and desires. Getting what you deserve was considered an indication of divine order and rightness. We get a sense of vindication, for instance, when Nicholas gets burned and Absalom farted on. We are also led to believe that the "rewards" each one gets are inevitable.

Test 2

| 1. C | 2. B | 3. B | 4. A | 5. A | 6. C |
| 7. B | 8. A | 9. C | 10. B | | |

11. For one thing, each wants what the other has: the old man wants the rioters' youth, and they want his knowledge, since they think he knows Death. The old man is also described as a "restless" wretch, a word that is also used in connection with the three rioters, who are forever searching for new amusements and debaucheries.

The old man expresses a willingness to exchange his worldly goods for a shroud, because he's lived long enough and wants to die. The young men do not realize that they will soon be doing just that, trading their new-found gold for shrouds, since the money the old man points them toward is indeed the embodiment of Death.

12. Without the Pardoner's shameless admission of the dirty tricks he plays on gullible villagers, we would just accept his tale as a moral fable against the excesses of greed, drunkenness, gluttony, and lechery. But he makes it clear that he feels no remorse for any of his evil deeds, so the tale takes on an added dimension of applying to the very person who's telling it. His exhortation to the pilgrims at the end to buy "relics" and contribute money, shows that he hasn't learned anything from the tale he's just told.

13. This can be answered on several levels. You can argue that Chanticleer, not being human, gives Chaucer and us a distance from his plight that allows us to see more clearly what Chaucer is saying about destiny and human nature. Also, look back at the end of the Chanticleer section. Chaucer uses humor, in this case a courtyard of chickens, to underline the fact that all things follow a natural order in which he has an unswerving faith.

Finally, animals and chickens do not, as a rule, undertake latenight discussions with their wives about the dreams they have or the workings of fate and destiny. Perhaps this is a way to get us to listen more closely to the points Chaucer is trying to make.

Term Paper Ideas

1. Why does Chaucer use a pilgrimage as a framework for the *Canterbury Tales?*

2. What is the importance of each character's station in life?

3. What are some examples of styles that Chaucer uses to tell the tales? Why are they effective?

4. How does the picture of Emelye bear on the idea of courtly love?

5. Why does Chaucer include all the descriptions of the battles and the building of the arena in the Knight's Tale?

6. Why does the Miller answer the Knight with a dirty story?

7. What can you tell about the Miller's view of religion from reading his Tale?

8. What does Nicholas' interest in astrology tell us about his character?

9. How does the Wife of Bath go against the religious and social conventions of her time?

10. Why does the Wife of Bath equate superiority in marriage with happiness?

11. What does the Pardoner's personality tell us about the tale he tells?

12. Why does the Pardoner use three rioters as examples of the people who go looking for Death?

13. How does the dream sequence in the Nun's Priest's Tale prepare us for the rest of the tale?

14. What support is there for the belief that the Nun's Priest and Chaucer are similar in outlook?

15. What does the use of classical styles tell us about Chanticleer and Pertelote?

Further Reading

Bowden, Muriel. *A Commentary of the General Prologue to the Canterbury Tales*. New York: Macmillan, 1967.

Chute, Marchette. *Geoffrey Chaucer of England*. New York: Dutton, 1958.

Coghill, Nevill. *The Poet Chaucer*. Oxford: Oxford University Press, 1949.

Donaldon, E. Talbot. *Speaking of Chaucer*. New York: Norton, 1970.

Dryden, John. *Selected Works*. New York: Holt, Rinehart and Winston, 1964.

Faulkner, Dewey R., ed. *Twentieth Century Interpretations of the Pardoner's Tale*. Englewood Cliffs, N.J.: Prentice-Hall, 1973.

Gardner, John. *The Poetry of Chaucer*. Carbondale, Ill.: Southern Illinois University Press, 1977.

Hussey, S. S. *Chaucer: An Introduction*, 2nd ed. London: Methuen, 1981.

Glossary

Here is a short glossary of the names that appear in the tales examined in this book.

Absalom The prissy, proper clerk in the Miller's Tale who is after Alison but can't get her.

Alison The wife of John the carpenter in the Miller's Tale, who is young and flirtatious and decides to sleep with Nicholas behind her husband's back.

Arcite One of the two knight "heroes" in the Knight's Tale, who gets released from prison and returns for the love of Emelye.

Boethius An early Christian philosopher who wrote *The Consolation of Philosophy*, which Chaucer translated, about the divine order that exists behind the swings of fortune.

Chanticleer The self-assured rooster hero of the Nun's Priest's Tale. He doesn't listen to his dreams and so gets carried away by a fox.

Emelye The object of desire in the Knight's Tale; Duke Theseus's sister-in-law.

Fortune Often personified as a fickle goddess, especially by Boethius, she raises people up or throws them down.

John The cuckolded carpenter in the Miller's Tale. He believes in God and in the astrology dupe that Nicholas pulls on him. (Also the name of the Nun's Priest.)

Mars God of war in the Knight's Tale, but also used to represent the planet Mars and its astrological influences. Arcite prays to Mars for victory.

Nicholas The "hende" (pleasant and sly) clerk of the Miller's Tale who concocts a scheme for John so that he can sleep with Alison.

Palamon The other young knight of the Knight's Tale, vying with his cousin Arcite for Emelye's love. He prays to Venus for victory.

Perotheus An old friend of Arcite's and Theseus' in the Knight's Tale, who intercedes to get Arcite sprung from prison.

Pertelote Chanticleer's lady love who doesn't believe in the psychic power of dreams.

Saturn The god and planet of doom and chaos in the Knight's Tale (and elsewhere in Chaucer). He arranges that Venus' knight, Palamon, shall win Emelye.

Thebes The ancient city where Arcite and Palamon are from. Theseus of Athens conquers Thebes by defeating the tyrant Creon.

Theseus Duke of Athens, conqueror of Thebes, he is the ruler who imprisons Arcite and Palamon, and later releases Arcite on Perotheus' request.

Venus The goddess of love. Her "day" is Friday, when the tournament takes place in the Knight's Tale, and when Chanticleer gets caught in the Nun's Priest's Tale. Both Palamon and Chanticleer are described as servants of Venus.

The Critics

On the General Prologue

To realize the exact extent of Chaucer's achievement in the Prologue to the *Canterbury Tales,* it is necessary to remember that the Middle Ages were not a time of portraits. It was a time of patterns, of allegories, of reducing the specific to the general and then drawing a moral from it. . . . What Chaucer was doing was entirely different. . . . He did not even set out to be entertaining. He merely set out to be accurate.

—*Marchette Chute,* Geoffrey Chaucer
of England, *1958*

Chaucer, like other debate narrators, takes no stand except in comic or ironic terms. . . . In all the tales, all human points of view have something to be said for them and something to be said against them.

—*John Gardner,* The Poetry of
Chaucer, *1977*

On the Characters

Chaucer's Knight is the personification of those [courtly] ideals, yet he is far more than the lay figure he would be were he that alone; like the other pilgrims taking this April journey to Canterbury, he is flesh and blood. He is one of those exceptional heroes who strive to live according to a great ideal yet who are at the same time understandably and understandingly human.

—*Muriel Bowden,* A Commentary on
the General Prologue to the
Canterbury Tales, 1969

The next pilgrim was the Wife of Bath, that lusty realist beside whom only Falstaff and Sancho Panza are worthy to walk. It is not until the lady swings into action that her remarkable qualities become evident, but even the brief portrait in the Prologue makes it clear that here is no ordinary woman.

—*Marchette Chute,* Geoffrey Chaucer
of England, *1958*

Chaucer knows his heroine [Alison] from her plucked eyebrows to the laces on her shoes. . . . He calls her a pet and a doll and a piggie's eye, and records with delight that she was softer than sheep's wool and prettier than a pear tree in bloom. He is charmed with her . . . and considers her so "gay a popelote" that the reader forgets, under Chaucer's brilliant and affectionate guidance, that she is only a common little flirt of a kind that could be duplicated by the dozen in any town in any century.

—*Marchette Chute*, Geoffrey Chaucer
of England, *1958*